BRONTË:
THE WORLD WITHOUT

ALSO BY JORDI MAND

Between the Sheets

BRONTË:
THE WORLD WITHOUT

JORDI MAND

PLAYWRIGHTS CANADA PRESS
TORONTO

For professional or amateur production rights, please contact:
Ian Arnold at Catalyst TCM
15 Old Primrose Lane, Toronto, ON M5A 4T1
416.568.8673 :: ian@catalysttcm.com

LIBRARY AND ARCHIVES CANADA CATALOGUING IN PUBLICATION
Title: Brontë : the world without / Jordi Mand.
Names: Mand, Jordi, author.
Description: First edition.
Identifiers: Canadiana (print) 20200198130 | Canadiana (ebook) 20200198157
  | ISBN 9780369101020 (softcover) | ISBN 9780369101037 (PDF)
  | ISBN 9780369101044 (EPUB) | ISBN 9780369101051 (Kindle)
Subjects: LCSH: Brontë, Anne, 1820-1849—Drama. | LCSH: Brontë, Charlotte,
  1816-1855—Drama. | LCSH: Brontë, Emily, 1818-1848—Drama. | LCGFT:
  Drama.
Classification: LCC PS8626.A519 B76 2020 | DDC C812/.6—dc23

Playwrights Canada Press operates on Mississaugas of the Credit, Wendat, Anishinaabe, Métis, and Haudenosaunee land. It always was and always will be Indigenous land.

We acknowledge the financial support of the Canada Council for the Arts—which last year invested $153 million to bring the arts to Canadians throughout the country—the Ontario Arts Council (OAC), Ontario Creates, and the Government of Canada for our publishing activities.

THREE SISTERS, STRIVING TO SUCCEED

But life is a battle: may we all be enabled to fight it well!
—Charlotte Brontë

Charlotte, Emily, and Anne Brontë were said to have described the world around them in two ways: there was the world within and the world without. The world within referred to their home and the walls of the parsonage they inhabited. It referred to the moors they spent so much of their life exploring. It referred to people they already knew and places they were familiar with. But so much of their lives actually revolved around what they referred to as the world without. A world they longed to be part of. A world with privileges that they did not have but that they craved. A world that dared them to become more than what they were.

Brontë: The World Without is my reimagining of who these women were. It's about what it means to want more from your life. It's about the pain and difficulties of being a family. It's about the joy and sacrifices of being an artist. It's about the complications and prejudices that come with being an ambitious woman. It's about what it means to love, to lose, to win, and to fail.

Charlotte, Emily, and Anne Brontë were born in England, between 1816 and 1820. Their mother died when they were young children, so their father, a prominent clergyman, primarily raised them. They were home-schooled after he learned of extremely poor conditions at the boarding school the girls were attending—conditions that had contributed to the early deaths of their elder sisters, Maria and Elizabeth.

Responsible for much of their education, Patrick Brontë recognized his daughters' love of storytelling and keen facility with language. Since women were not encouraged to speak or write freely at the time, his attitude largely helped to shape who they would later become. The sisters, along with their brother, Branwell, spent much of their youth creating stories.

While their father was a beloved leader in the religious community, they struggled financially. The sisters went on to train professionally as governesses—a profession in which women were often treated terribly. They took work when they could to help ensure the family had the means to survive.

Branwell was a talented portrait artist who the family hoped would go on to make a name for himself. Over time, it became clear that he would never be able to shoulder any financial responsibility. Feeling increasingly anxious about their family's financial state, Charlotte, Emily, and Anne stumbled upon an ingenious way to make money while propelling their professional pursuits forward. And it's here that my play begins: at a pivotal time in their lives when their artistic endeavours began to shift, solidify, and take off.

One of the ongoing sources of inspiration for me in writing about these remarkable women is the reminder of how truly modern they were.

As artists, they wrote in a way that depicted what society was like when they were alive—specifically, how white women of their class were treated. They created heroines who were smart and industrious. Their stories showcased the vulnerability of women in their society and gave voice to concerns that were not being discussed. The relationships they depicted outwardly challenged the power dynamics of women and men. They wrote about what interested them and were not concerned with populism.

They were resilient, entrepreneurial, and ambitious. They came to understand that they would have to take their destiny into their own hands in order to see their dreams fulfilled. They were utterly determined to make something of their lives and use their talents to the fullest. They also had to deal with the fear and doubt that comes from trying to pursue greatness. They were forced to face rejection—over and over again. Despite how successful they were, each had to deal with failure in her own way.

As women, they dealt with the ongoing difficulty of pursuing their vocation while managing a household. They challenged the standards of marriage and expectations of child-bearing within their race and social class when to do so did not even occur to most women. They lived their lives knowing full well that writing was not an encouraged profession.

As sisters, they were one another's greatest support system and fiercest competition. They were witnesses to each other's heartbreaks, accomplishments, failures, and losses. They were bound together by the tragedies of their family—having lost their mother, aunt, and two older sisters. They stood by each other as they cared for their father, brother, and one another.

I have been moved by their tenacity and desire. I have been stirred by their words and their world. I have been touched by their profound bond and connection with one another. It has been my honour to write about these astonishing women.

Jordi Mand
Spring 2020

NOTES ON THE PLAY

Within the story some historical events have been condensed, combined, and adapted for dramatic purposes.

Though this play is set in England, the dialogue is written to be played without English accents.

Diversity in casting is strongly encouraged.

The play can be performed with or without an intermission. If an intermission is included, it should come at the end of Movement 2.

The feeling of the prelude, interludes, and postlude should be quite different from the movements. The interludes exist almost more like choreography. Lights, sounds, and staging should be used to convey the feeling of time passing between the movements, to develop relationships, to evoke the emotional and creative lives of the characters, and to show important moments in their journeys.

A dash indicates when a character is being cut off by another character.

An ellipsis indicates when a character stops themselves or has a change in thought.

Brontë: The World Without was first produced by the Stratford Festival at the Studio Theatre in Stratford, Ontario, from June 30 to October 13, 2018, with the following cast and creative team:

Charlotte Brontë: Beryl Bain
Emily Brontë: Jessica B. Hill
Anne Brontë: Andrea Rankin

Director: Vanessa Porteous
Dramaturg: Bob White
Set and Costume Designer: Narda McCarroll
Lighting Designer: Kimberly Purtell
Sound Designer: Anton de Groot
Stage Manager: Kim Lott
Assistant Stage Manager: Katherine Dermott
Fight Director: John Stead
Assistant Designer: Alison Marshall
Assistant Lighting Designers: Frank Donato and Imogen Wilson
Associate Fight Director: Anita Nittoly
Production Assistant: Nyssa Beairsto
Production Stage Managers: Marie Fewer-Muncic and Angela Marshall
Technical Director: Sean Hirtle

CHARACTERS

Charlotte Brontë
Emily Brontë
Anne Brontë

TIMELINE

Movement 1: January 1846
Movement 2: October 1846
Movement 3: July 1847
Movement 4: September 1848
Movement 5: January 1849

PRELUDE

A room in an older house. The house sits on top of a hill with a graveyard at the foot of the property.

The room itself has two large windows without curtains. There is a bookshelf filled with books. On one wall is a working fireplace, tables with various trinkets on it, and a framed landscape painting. Against another wall is a sofa with a cushion. There is also a rocking chair. In the middle of the room is a table with chairs around it. On the table are three lit candles, three sewing boxes, and three writing desks.

The room appears to be in order but should feel lived in. The space functions as a dining room, living room, and drawing room within the house.

The sound of a clock tolls throughout the house.

MOVEMENT 1

Evening.

CHARLOTTE, twenty-nine, sits at the table. She sews, holding her work close to her face. EMILY, twenty-seven, sits on the sofa, staring into the night. ANNE, twenty-five, sits in the rocking chair, sewing quickly. All three women are dressed for bed.

EMILY puts her sewing down, grabs a candle, then leaves the room without acknowledging the other two.

ANNE puts her needle into her sewing box. She gathers EMILY's sewing and tries to collect CHARLOTTE's sewing, but CHARLOTTE resists.

CHARLOTTE   I can put it away myself.

ANNE   We've been keeping the sewing upstairs.

CHARLOTTE   Why not keep it in the basket?

ANNE   I've been working on some larger pieces. She doesn't like it when I leave it on the floor.

CHARLOTTE   That's why we keep it in the—

CHARLOTTE looks around the room.

Where is the basket?

ANNE Upstairs. It's been easier to just—

CHARLOTTE Fine. Fine. Do what you like.

CHARLOTTE hands ANNE her sewing. ANNE heads for the door. As she does, she stubs her toe.

ANNE Owww.

CHARLOTTE Anne.

ANNE Owww, owww, owww, owww. Owww.

CHARLOTTE Anne. Shhh.

ANNE I'm trying, but . . . Owww. My toe.

ANNE leaves, limping.

EMILY enters carrying a tray with a teapot and three teacups. She places the tray on the table and pours tea into the cups. EMILY hands CHARLOTTE a cup. CHARLOTTE sips, then makes a face.

CHARLOTTE It's weak.

EMILY We don't have very much left. Do you want me to steep it longer?

ANNE enters.

CHARLOTTE	No. No. It's fine.
ANNE	Is there enough for me?
EMILY	Yes. But there's only enough left for one more—
ANNE	Make sure you pour me a full cup.
EMILY	Why wouldn't I pour you a full—
ANNE	Sometimes you give me less than—
EMILY	When?
ANNE	Sometimes you—
EMILY	No. I never—
CHARLOTTE	Can we begin?

They look at each other, then sit at the table.

Well?

EMILY and ANNE exchange a look.

ANNE	You go.
EMILY	No. You.
ANNE	You.
EMILY	You.
ANNE	Emily!

EMILY	Anne!
CHARLOTTE	Will one of you please just—
EMILY	All right!

Beat.

Tabby won't be returning.

CHARLOTTE	She won't be returning at all or she won't be returning—
EMILY	She isn't well enough to work yet. Her brother wrote to us last week. They don't know when she'll be able to come back.
ANNE	She should have stayed here . . . With us. We could have cared for her.
EMILY	She wanted to be with her family.
ANNE	We are her family.
CHARLOTTE	No, we're her employers. You're still taking on her duties?
EMILY	Martha's been here once a week but mainly . . . Yes. It's been me.

ANNE clears her throat.

Anne's been helping since she returned.

ANNE	I keep asking her to let me do more. She hardly lets me—
EMILY	You create more work for me.

ANNE	No.
EMILY	Yes. Your ironing? You burnt my dress.
ANNE	That was an accident.
EMILY	It's easier if I just do it myself.
CHARLOTTE	What have you been doing these past few weeks if you're not helping her?
ANNE	I've been looking after Papa.
CHARLOTTE	How long has he had the cough?
ANNE	A week or two.
CHARLOTTE	You called for a doctor?
EMILY	We did.
ANNE	Emily didn't want me to.
EMILY	I thought we should have waited a little longer before we—
ANNE	And I thought he was doing poorly enough to call.
CHARLOTTE	You haven't seen any improvement?
EMILY	His fever's gone down. Now he's just weak.
ANNE	He's had very little appetite. He hasn't had a full meal in days.
CHARLOTTE	That's why he's weak. He needs to eat.

ANNE	I've tried to get him to eat. He won't let me.
CHARLOTTE	You have to try harder.
ANNE	You try forcing him to do something he doesn't want to do.
CHARLOTTE	You have to insist.
ANNE	I do. He refuses. It takes all my strength not to take the spoon and shove it down his throat myself.
EMILY	Anne!
ANNE	Everything's a challenge with him. And he's been in a miserable mood.
CHARLOTTE	Have you heard from Branwell?
EMILY	No. Has he written to you?
CHARLOTTE	No. Have you heard from him?
ANNE	Why would I hear from him?
CHARLOTTE	The two of you used to see each other every day.
ANNE	Not every day.
CHARLOTTE	You saw one another for suppers.
ANNE	We took meals at different times.
CHARLOTTE	You wrote me and said that you and Bran spent all your time together—

ANNE   When he first arrived at the Robinsons' . . . Yes. But that didn't last. Before long we would go for months without talking to each other. He mainly talked to . . .

ANNE looks at them, then stops herself.

I hardly saw him.

CHARLOTTE   I'll write to him to ask when he'll be visiting next.

ANNE chuckles.

What?

ANNE   Nothing.

CHARLOTTE   You don't think I should ask him when he intends to—

ANNE   I don't think he'll be visiting any time soon.

CHARLOTTE   Did he say something to make you think he—

ANNE   I told you . . . He hardly spoke to me. He wouldn't even see me off the day I left.

CHARLOTTE   Well, did you do something to upset him or—

ANNE   No, Charlotte. I didn't do anything. If you want an explanation . . . Ask him yourself.

ANNE heads for the door.

CHARLOTTE   Anne.

ANNE stops.

ANNE	What?
CHARLOTTE	We need to finish. Sit.
ANNE	Can't we do this in the morning?
CHARLOTTE	The purpose of us speaking tonight was to—
ANNE	I thought the purpose was for us to be together.
CHARLOTTE	That was part of it. But more pressing is—
EMILY	Anne . . .

EMILY indicates for ANNE to join them. ANNE walks to the table, but decides not to sit with her sisters. She walks to the rocking chair and plops herself down.

CHARLOTTE	She listens to you. But with me . . . She won't even—
ANNE	I can hear you.
CHARLOTTE	Well, you won't come when I call.
ANNE	I'm not a dog, Charlotte.
CHARLOTTE	I'm not saying you're a—
EMILY	Shhh . . .

EMILY looks toward the door.

CHARLOTTE	How much do we have?

EMILY opens a small notebook, then hands it to
CHARLOTTE.

That's all?

EMILY   Yes.

CHARLOTTE   What about Papa's salary?

EMILY   That's with the salary.

CHARLOTTE   You're certain?

EMILY   Yes. We counted everything.

CHARLOTTE   This is with Auntie's inheritance?

EMILY   No.

CHARLOTTE   Why wouldn't you include that?

EMILY   That money is for our future.

ANNE   And she only left us a very small amount.

EMILY   She would never forgive us if we used it now . . . For the household.

CHARLOTTE   Well, there doesn't seem to be enough.

ANNE   Because there isn't.

CHARLOTTE   This will hardly get us through until the end of winter.

                 Beat.

	How much were you able to save from the Robinsons?
ANNE	It's there.
CHARLOTTE	How much?
ANNE	Fifteen pounds.
EMILY	Most of what we have is Anne's.
ANNE	We've used as little as possible since I've returned.
EMILY	And you? How much were you able to save from Brussels?
CHARLOTTE	After paying for my classes, books, paper, quills, postage, my travel home—
EMILY	But they paid you when you started to teach there.
CHARLOTTE	Teaching meant I was there longer than we had originally—
EMILY	Did you save anything?
CHARLOTTE	A few pounds.
ANNE	How much is a few?
CHARLOTTE	Three. Three pounds.

EMILY and ANNE look at each other.

I tried to save more. It wasn't possible. They didn't pay me enough to . . .

Beat.

	Have you told Papa?
EMILY	No. Not yet.
ANNE	We didn't want to worry him.
EMILY	And we wanted to wait . . . Until you returned.
CHARLOTTE	Why? So I could be the one to tell him?
EMILY	So we could decide together how best to proceed.
CHARLOTTE	What about Branwell? We need to tell him, at least.
ANNE	Why?
CHARLOTTE	Considering he's the only one of us who's actually employed.
ANNE	We'll see how long that lasts.
CHARLOTTE	Anne!
ANNE	What? He's been fired from every post he's ever had.
CHARLOTTE	Bran needs to know. I'll include it in my letter to him. I'll ask him how much he's saved since starting at the Robinsons'.
ANNE	He hasn't saved anything.
CHARLOTTE	We don't know that.
ANNE	He's never been good with money.
CHARLOTTE	He's been good at making it.

ANNE   No. He's been good at spending it.

CHARLOTTE   Maybe he can send something in the meantime. Something
                small, even to . . .

                *EMILY takes the notebook from CHARLOTTE. She flips to
                a new page, then hands it back to CHARLOTTE.*

                (*reading*) Coffee, tea, beef, sugar, salt, flour, oats, potatoes,
                beans, peas, cabbage, celery, butter, raisins, and bacon.

EMILY   We're running low . . . On all of it.

CHARLOTTE   We don't need coffee.

                CHARLOTTE grabs for a pencil.

ANNE   Papa drinks it.

CHARLOTTE   He shouldn't. It's hard on his system.

ANNE   He asks us to serve it when he has visitors.

EMILY   And Bran would want some if he were here.

CHARLOTTE   We don't need bacon.

ANNE   Yes.

CHARLOTTE   It's not necessary for us to have bacon in the—

ANNE   I love bacon.

                CHARLOTTE crosses bacon off the list.

CHARLOTTE	We don't need beef.
ANNE	Papa needs it. The doctor said. He needs it for his health.
CHARLOTTE	He hates the taste of meat. And it's too hard for him to digest.
ANNE	He needs it to keep up his strength.
CHARLOTTE	Well if he isn't eating—
EMILY	Perhaps we can buy a small portion for Papa. The three of us can do without.
CHARLOTTE	Yes. We'll buy beans instead.

CHARLOTTE writes in the notebook. ANNE rolls her eyes.

We don't need cabbage and celery. Cabbage seems to be of more use to us . . . Yes?

EMILY	Yes.
ANNE	Yes.

CHARLOTTE makes another note. She sees the candles on the table and blows one of them out.

CHARLOTTE	What? It's an expense.
ANNE	That's hardly going to—
CHARLOTTE	We have to start somewhere. We can dismiss Martha.
EMILY	No.

CHARLOTTE   If she's only here once a week—

EMILY   I can't take care of the entire house on my own.

CHARLOTTE   I thought Anne was helping.

EMILY   She is. But not enough to—

ANNE   I help.

CHARLOTTE   I'm simply looking for a way to—

EMILY   It's too much for one person.

CHARLOTTE   Well, something has to change. Something has to . . .

> CHARLOTTE *rubs her eyes.*

We'll let Martha go this week.

ANNE   But she's so sweet. She's my—

CHARLOTTE   That's not a reason to pay her to do something we can do ourselves.

> CHARLOTTE *looks at them.*

You didn't tell me it had gotten so . . .

> CHARLOTTE *sees* EMILY *and* ANNE *look at each other.*

What?

ANNE   You tell her.

EMILY	No. You.
ANNE	Emily.
EMILY	I already told her about the—
CHARLOTTE	Tell me what?

Beat.

EMILY	Papa, he's . . . He's losing his sight.
CHARLOTTE	Does he need new glasses?
EMILY	No. It's not that.
CHARLOTTE	Did you ask the doctor? What did he say when he—
EMILY	He's going blind.

Beat.

CHARLOTTE	Blind?

Beat.

EMILY	There's a surgery . . . A procedure. It could help restore his sight.

ANNE goes to her writing desk. She pulls out a newspaper clipping and hands it to CHARLOTTE.

CHARLOTTE	Fully?
EMILY	No. Not fully.

ANNE   Almost fully.

EMILY   It would make a difference. He would be able to walk on his
              own . . . Read on his own. He wouldn't need help getting
              up and down from the pulpit during services.

CHARLOTTE   Has Papa seen this?

ANNE   He's the one who showed it to us.

CHARLOTTE   And because of one article he thinks this will actually—

EMILY   Charlotte . . . He fell.

CHARLOTTE   When?

EMILY   A few weeks ago.

ANNE   After services.

EMILY   He fell down the stairs . . . In front of the entire congrega-
              tion. He was mortified.

CHARLOTTE   Why did you wait until now to tell me?

EMILY   He asked us not to tell you . . . You or Bran. He didn't want
              to cause a scene.

CHARLOTTE   Was he hurt?

EMILY   Yes.

ANNE   He cut his head. Sprained his wrist. He was shaking for days.

EMILY	He thinks he may lose his position if he doesn't have the surgery.
CHARLOTTE	He's given years of his life to this community. They wouldn't do that.
EMILY	It doesn't matter. If he can't see they'll bring in another priest to replace him. And there won't be any need for him here.
	He would lose his job.
ANNE	And we would lose our home.
CHARLOTTE	We wouldn't. They would find some way for us to stay here . . . For Papa to stay, certainly.
EMILY	How? We have no ownership here. If he's dismissed we'll be forced to leave.
ANNE	And we would have nowhere to go. We can't afford bacon, never mind a home to—
CHARLOTTE	All right. All right.
	Beat.
	Where would he have the surgery done?
EMILY	In Manchester.
CHARLOTTE	That's a day's journey.
EMILY	He's eager to go.
CHARLOTTE	How soon would he have to leave?

EMILY   As soon as we can pay for it.

CHARLOTTE   How much is it going to cost?

EMILY   Ten pounds.

CHARLOTTE   Ten pounds? And we don't even know if it will be successful?

EMILY   We don't have any reason to think it won't be.

CHARLOTTE   We'd have to stay in Manchester while he recovered. That will add to the cost.

EMILY   We know.

> *Beat.*

We'd want you to take him.

CHARLOTTE   I just returned.

EMILY   You wouldn't have to go until we had the money.

CHARLOTTE   This is all so . . .

> *Beat.*

I was hoping to be here . . . For a while. To be at home . . . With Papa . . . With the two of you before I . . .

> *Beat.*

How are we going to . . .

> *Beat.*

ANNE	What if we sold some things? To help with the cost of—
EMILY	What would we sell?
ANNE	I don't know . . . Books.
CHARLOTTE	We're not selling our books.
ANNE	Why not? We've read them all. We can take them out from the library if we want to read them again.
CHARLOTTE	Papa would never let us sell them.
ANNE	He doesn't have to know.
CHARLOTTE	He would figure it out when he came looking for something to read.
ANNE	We have furniture. Some pieces in the kitchen we could—
EMILY	Those pieces were Mama's.
ANNE	She isn't using them.
EMILY	Anne!
CHARLOTTE	For goodness' sake!
ANNE	She isn't. Mama would want them to go to good use. We have dishes, serving plates, cutlery.
EMILY	Those are the only possessions of hers we have left.
ANNE	No. We have her jewellery.

CHARLOTTE	We're not selling Mama's things.
ANNE	The piano then. We could make a fortune off it.
EMILY	No. It was a gift from Papa.
ANNE	Think of how much we could make if we—
EMILY	I play it. I play it every day. We're not selling the piano.
ANNE	I don't hear either of you contributing.
CHARLOTTE	How do you think it would look if we started selling off every item we have? We don't want the congregation to think that Papa was in such need that—
ANNE	What about Branwell's paintings? We could sell those, couldn't we? How much could we make for this one?

ANNE goes to the painting above the fireplace.

CHARLOTTE	How would we even go about selling his paintings? Bran's the only one of us who knows anything about—
EMILY	He could help. Perhaps he could even paint us a couple of new ones.
ANNE	If we want something new, Charlotte should paint them. You're as good a painter as he is. Both of you are.
CHARLOTTE	No. We're not skilled like he is. When I write him, I'll inform him of our situation and—
ANNE	We shouldn't rely on him.

EMILY	We've helped him on countless occasions. We saved everything we could to send him to school.
ANNE	We should never have sent him to school in the first place. He's not even using his training.
CHARLOTTE	At least he's working.
ANNE	As a tutor. Not as a painter.
CHARLOTTE	It takes time to develop a career of that—
ANNE	And in that time we may freeze and starve to death.
CHARLOTTE	We won't freeze.
ANNE	You don't know that.
CHARLOTTE	Anne. We're not going to—
ANNE	What about our school then?

Beat.

CHARLOTTE	We never found enough students to make it work.
ANNE	Couldn't we try again?
CHARLOTTE	In the time it would take to set everything up we'd run out of money. The costs alone of turning this house into a school—
ANNE	We could use our inheritance.
EMILY	That money is for—

ANNE	For our future . . . Yes. But wouldn't Auntie feel that turning our home into a school for girls is the very best use of her money?
CHARLOTTE	Papa can hardly stand us in the house, never mind a house full of girls he doesn't know.
ANNE	What was the point of sending you to Brussels if—
EMILY	Anne—
ANNE	You went there to learn new skills to be able to come back here to teach.
CHARLOTTE	I know why I went.
ANNE	So? If we looked at opening the school again maybe we could—
CHARLOTTE	Anne . . . It won't happen.
ANNE	But if we tried . . . Maybe we could—
CHARLOTTE	Anne!

Beat.

I'll put an ad in the paper.

EMILY	For?
CHARLOTTE	For me . . . To be a governess.
EMILY	I thought you wanted to be at home.

CHARLOTTE   We can't afford for me to be at home.

EMILY   We need you to take Papa for his surgery.

CHARLOTTE   And first we need money so he can afford to have the surgery at all.

EMILY   I could look for something.

CHARLOTTE   No. You can't.

EMILY   I could try.

CHARLOTTE   You would be miserable.

EMILY   So would you.

CHARLOTTE   Emily . . . Every time you leave you get sick.

EMILY   Not every time.

CHARLOTTE
/ ANNE   Yes!

CHARLOTTE   Every single time. You can barely walk out the front door without getting homesick. I'll put an ad in the paper this week.

ANNE   So will I.

EMILY   Both of you? What about the house?

CHARLOTTE   We need the money more than you need the help.

ANNE   Can't you teach?

CHARLOTTE   There aren't any teaching positions in the area.

ANNE   You're sure?

CHARLOTTE   Yes. I sent letters to whomever I could. There's nothing.

EMILY   Can't you return to Brussels? The Hégers would gladly have you back.

CHARLOTTE   No. I don't think they would.

EMILY   Yes. Monsieur Héger would want you to go back. You were Monsieur Héger's favourite student.

CHARLOTTE   I can't. I can't go back.

EMILY   Have they found someone to replace you?

CHARLOTTE   Even if they haven't . . . There's nothing for me there.

EMILY   There's a job for you there.

CHARLOTTE   No. I can't go back. I can't spend another moment at that school . . . In that place. I simply . . .

    Beat.

    I don't want to teach.

ANNE   Why would you dream of opening a school of your own if you don't want to—

CHARLOTTE   Because it was something we could have done together. Something that could have been ours. We wouldn't have to leave home. We wouldn't have to work for another family and be treated like servants.

Beat.

The Sidgwicks expected me to care for the children and clean the house and tend to the kitchen. I was governess, maid, and all. Once their son hit me in the head with a Bible and I was the one reprimanded.

ANNE   The Robinsons' son used to force me to go outside with him to hunt for nests. When he found one . . . His greatest pleasure was ripping the legs and wings off every little bird he could find. I've never met a more despicable child in all my life.

CHARLOTTE   I hate children.

ANNE   I hate children.

EMILY   You love children.

ANNE   No. Children love me. There's a difference.

Beat.

EMILY   Isn't there anything else we could do?

CHARLOTTE   What? What else could we do?

Beat.

EMILY   What if you receive a response?

CHARLOTTE   Then we'll take the work.

EMILY   Both of you?

CHARLOTTE   Emily, we can't refuse it. Not now.

EMILY   And if neither of you receives a response . . . What then?

               Beat.

               They look at each other.

INTERLUDE

CHARLOTTE, EMILY, and ANNE *tidy the room.*

EMILY *collects the tray, teacups, and two of the candles. She leaves.*

CHARLOTTE *looks through their book collection. She decides what to give away., then she hands the books to* ANNE, *who leaves.*

CHARLOTTE *looks at the trinkets on the tables.* ANNE *enters and takes the painting down from above the fireplace.*

CHARLOTTE *hands some of the trinkets to* ANNE, *who leaves with the trinkets and painting.*

CHARLOTTE *notices paper sticking out of* EMILY's *writing desk. She opens the desk and looks through it, finding a small notebook that she reads.*

EMILY *enters. She sees* CHARLOTTE *reading her work and rushes to her, grabbing the notebook from* CHARLOTTE *and running out of the room.*

ANNE enters. She starts to tidy the room. CHARLOTTE *joins her.* EMILY *enters.* CHARLOTTE *moves toward* EMILY *to say something, but* EMILY *quickly moves away from her and leaves.*

CHARLOTTE *and* ANNE *reorganize the chairs around the table. They both grab their sewing. They sit. And work.*

MOVEMENT 2

Evening. Nine months later.

CHARLOTTE, thirty, sits at the table sewing. ANNE, twenty-six, sits in the rocking chair sewing. They are dressed for bed.

ANNE stands. She pours tea in the three teacups. She hands CHARLOTTE a cup and takes one for herself. She contemplates sitting beside CHARLOTTE, but decides to sit back in the rocking chair.

The front door to the house is opened then closed quickly. CHARLOTTE and ANNE look at each other.

EMILY, twenty-eight, enters wearing a day dress and cloak.

CHARLOTTE   Where have you been?

EMILY   I needed to walk.

CHARLOTTE   You already went out this afternoon.

EMILY   I needed to walk again.

EMILY goes to her writing desk. She opens it to make sure nothing is missing, then slams it shut.

I'm going to bed.

CHARLOTTE   You never go to bed this early.

EMILY   I'm tired.

CHARLOTTE   Emily.

EMILY   Good night.

EMILY heads for the door. CHARLOTTE stands.

CHARLOTTE   We agreed to speak about Branwell.

EMILY   We can speak about Branwell in the morning.

CHARLOTTE   He'll be awake in the morning.

ANNE   He's been here a week already and hasn't risen before noon since he—

EMILY   See? We'll have plenty of time to talk about him tomorrow.

CHARLOTTE runs to the door before EMILY can get to it, preventing her from leaving. EMILY tries to sneak past CHARLOTTE.

Charlotte.

CHARLOTTE prevents EMILY from going.

Enough.

EMILY tries to sneak past CHARLOTTE again.

Let me go.

EMILY pushes CHARLOTTE out of the way.

CHARLOTTE   How long are you going to carry on like this? She's barely spoken to me in days.

ANNE   I know. I know.

EMILY   You should have thought about that before you decided to—

CHARLOTTE   I didn't decide anything. I found it. And now you'd rather hide in your room—

EMILY   I'm not hiding.

CHARLOTTE   Instead of discussing your brother's future. Discussing . . . together . . . How we can help him.

EMILY   He doesn't want our help.

CHARLOTTE   He doesn't know what he wants.

ANNE   He shouldn't have come here.

CHARLOTTE   And where do you propose he should have gone instead?

ANNE   To stay with a friend . . . or anyone else.

CHARLOTTE   He's in no condition to stay with anyone else.

ANNE   He's in no condition to stay here either.

CHARLOTTE   If you had just told us . . . Warned us that he was—

ANNE   He wasn't like this at the Robinsons'. He wasn't stumbling around . . . Drunk at all hours of the night—

CHARLOTTE   How could you not tell us about . . . I can't even bring myself to say her name. How could you not—

ANNE   I didn't know.

CHARLOTTE   Anne! You lived in the same house as them.

ANNE   And they were careful . . . Cautious. I had my suspicions . . . Of course I did. But I never thought they were actually—

CHARLOTTE   How could he do this? They were his employers. She was his . . .

    Beat.

He has to apologize.

EMILY   To who?

CHARLOTTE   To Mr. Robinson. He should be begging that man for forgiveness. Offering him anything he can to—

ANNE   What does Bran have to offer him?

CHARLOTTE   He could work without pay.

EMILY   Branwell must never come into contact with the Robinsons again.

CHARLOTTE   Something has to be done.

EMILY	He needs to stay in bed. He needs to recover.
ANNE	Recover from drinking night after night?
EMILY	Well, if we let him drink in the house like I suggested—
CHARLOTTE	No. He's not drinking in the house.
EMILY	He's going to drink one way or another. We might as well let him—
CHARLOTTE	If he's so intent on destroying himself . . . He can do that on his own . . . Outside of this house.
ANNE	He needs a doctor.
EMILY	He needs time. He's grieving.
CHARLOTTE	Grieving?
EMILY	I believe him when he says he loves her. He said they intended to marry.
CHARLOTTE	She's already married, Emily . . . To someone else.
EMILY	She was going to leave her husband.
CHARLOTTE	Do you really think that a woman like that . . . Who would behave in that way . . . In her own home . . . Would leave her husband for a man without a single penny to his name? She was never going to leave him. And now our lives are ruined.

They hear a loud noise above them.

What was that?

EMILY goes to the door as if to leave.

No. Anne . . . Go see what it is.

ANNE   Why do I always have to be the one to—

CHARLOTTE   Anne!

ANNE looks at them, then leaves. EMILY goes to follow.

Where are you going?

EMILY   With Anne.

CHARLOTTE   Emily.

EMILY   What?

CHARLOTTE   This distance between us . . . I can't stand it. I've forgiven
              you. Why can't you forgive me?

EMILY   Forgiven me? For what?

CHARLOTTE   For reading my letter.

EMILY   I made myself perfectly clear . . . If you continued to write
              to Monsieur Héger . . . I would open any letter I found in
              the house. You had no business writing to him.

CHARLOTTE   I had to try and reach him again. To see if he at least—

EMILY   He asked you not to contact him.

CHARLOTTE	Reading that letter from him was the most excruciating . . .

Beat.

I needed to know if he—

EMILY heads for the door.

Emily . . . Please.

EMILY closes the door, then returns to CHARLOTTE. She pulls CHARLOTTE to the sofa to sit with her.

EMILY	He's married. He has a wife . . . And a family.
CHARLOTTE	I know.
EMILY	He has a respectable position at a respected school. You shouldn't have allowed yourself to think that anything would come of it.
CHARLOTTE	I know. I thought that he . . .

Beat.

I know how foolish it is.

EMILY	Do you?
CHARLOTTE	Yes. But I couldn't . . .

Beat.

I had to write him again. I had to know if there was any chance that our friendship—

EMILY	Friendship?
CHARLOTTE	I had to know if there was any way for me to keep him in my life. To keep him . . .

    Beat.

    He was so kind to me.

EMILY	Many people have been kind to you, Charlotte.
CHARLOTTE	Not like him. He took such care with me.
EMILY	You were his student.
CHARLOTTE	But the way he spoke to me . . . The way he treated me . . . The gifts he gave me. He favoured me over everyone else at that school.
EMILY	That doesn't mean he had affectionate—
CHARLOTTE	Then what? What does it mean?

    Beat.

    You don't know what it's like. To feel that way for another—

EMILY	I can imagine.
CHARLOTTE	Imagining is not the same.

    Beat.

EMILY	I'm going to check on Anne.

EMILY heads for the door.

CHARLOTTE I can't stand the idea of losing you too.

EMILY You haven't lost me.

CHARLOTTE It certainly feels that way.

EMILY Charlotte . . . What you read . . . These are some of my most private . . . My most private . . . They were never meant for anyone to read.

CHARLOTTE How could I not read them? They're too extraordinary not to—

EMILY They aren't for you . . . They aren't for anyone other than myself.

ANNE enters.

CHARLOTTE What was it?

ANNE Papa. He fell.

CHARLOTTE Again?

EMILY Is he all right?

ANNE He missed the edge of the bed. He needs to have the surgery.

CHARLOTTE We don't have enough saved yet to be able to afford—

ANNE We've been saving for almost a year.

EMILY And we still don't have enough.

ANNE	We'll use our inheritance then.
EMILY	Our inheritance is hardly enough to—
ANNE	What were you fighting about?
EMILY	It was . . . Nothing.
CHARLOTTE	It wasn't nothing.
EMILY	Charlotte.
CHARLOTTE	Emily's upset with me for finding some of her writing. And I'm trying to apologize but she refuses to—
EMILY	I don't hear an actual apology, Charlotte.
ANNE	You don't let anyone read your writing.
EMILY	I didn't let her read it. She took it . . . Without asking.
CHARLOTTE	I didn't take anything. I stumbled across it and—
EMILY	No. You were looking. You always have to know everything.
CHARLOTTE	That isn't true.
EMILY	How many times have you been behind that door listening to our conversations? Private conversations that—
ANNE	What did you write?
CHARLOTTE	She's written some of the most—
EMILY	Stop it—

CHARLOTTE	Emily . . . Your work is stunning. It's not like any poetry I've ever read.
EMILY	It's not poetry. They're a few rhymes. That's all.
CHARLOTTE	Your words . . . They're haunting—
EMILY	Enough.
CHARLOTTE	Filled with the deepest sense of—
EMILY	Please . . . I'm begging you. Can we forget you ever found them? That you ever . . .

Beat.

These are my most . . . They were never meant to be read . . . They were never meant to be—

ANNE	I want to know what you're talking about.
EMILY	Have you not been listening? They're not for you. For either of you.

EMILY's breathing changes.

You should never have . . .

EMILY grabs her chest.

You will not read any more . . . You will respect my privacy. Do you hear me? You will not read any more . . .

EMILY gasps for air.

ANNE   I'll get a cloth.

> *ANNE leaves. EMILY stumbles and falls to the ground. She breathes heavily. CHARLOTTE goes to her.*

CHARLOTTE   It's all right. You're all right.

> *EMILY struggles to breathe.*

Take a breath. Can you do that? Like this.

> *CHARLOTTE takes a breath. EMILY tries to copy her. CHARLOTTE moves behind EMILY and holds her tightly so EMILY can feel her breathing.*

Again. With me.

> *EMILY takes another breath. ANNE enters with a small basin and cloth. She rings out the cloth.*

Calm. Calm.

> *ANNE places the cloth on EMILY's forehead.*

Good.

> *EMILY takes the cloth from ANNE. She holds it tightly against her face. Her breath slowly becomes steadier.*

Do you want to stand?

> *EMILY shakes her head.*

ANNE   We should call for the doctor.

EMILY	No. We can't afford—
CHARLOTTE	If you need someone, we'll find a way to—
EMILY	No. No. It's . . .

EMILY takes a deep breath.

It will pass.

Beat.

CHARLOTTE	Do you want some tea?

EMILY shakes her head.

Something to eat?

EMILY shakes her head.

ANNE	Are you sure? We have honey cake left from when Mr. Nicholls came to visit.

Beat.

EMILY	All right.
ANNE	Charlotte, do you want some—
CHARLOTTE	Yes. Yes. Bring whatever's left.

ANNE leaves. EMILY tries to stand.

Slowly.

EMILY moves slowly. She sits on the sofa and grabs her chest. Her breathing hasn't fully normalized yet. CHARLOTTE watches EMILY closely.

ANNE enters with a tray that has a large plate covered by a cloth and three smaller plates.

ANNE Don't tell Papa if we finish it. Honey cake is his favourite.

CHARLOTTE We can blame it on Bran.

ANNE Yes! Let's blame it on Bran!

ANNE places the tray on the table, removes the cloth, and reveals a small section of cake.

Oh . . . I thought we had more.

CHARLOTTE Looks like Bran got to it after all.

ANNE There's hardly enough for three slices.

CHARLOTTE Give Emily a larger piece.

EMILY I don't need a larger piece.

ANNE I'll take it then.

EMILY I was being polite. I'll take a larger piece.

ANNE cuts the cake and gives each of them a slice. EMILY immediately begins to devour it. CHARLOTTE and ANNE watch her. They laugh.

CHARLOTTE Slow down. You'll choke.

EMILY looks at them and slows down. They hear a noise in the hallway.

ANNE   Papa?

ANNE stands, goes to the door, and opens it slightly. They hear someone belch loudly. ANNE closes the door quickly.

CHARLOTTE   No. Not Papa.

They hear the front door to the house being opened then slammed shut. They breathe a sigh of relief. ANNE sits at the table and takes a bite of the cake.

ANNE   It's too dry.

CHARLOTTE   I don't think so.

EMILY, who has already finished her piece, reaches for ANNE's plate and starts to eat her cake.

Neither does she.

CHARLOTTE and ANNE laugh.

Beat.

ANNE goes to her writing desk and pulls out a notebook. In the notebook are several loose pieces of paper.

ANNE looks them over, then decides to hand them to CHARLOTTE.

What?

CHARLOTTE holds the pages close to her face. And reads.

Where did you get these from?

ANNE   I wrote them.

(to EMILY) I changed the order of the first few lines . . . Like
you said.

CHARLOTTE   You've read these?

EMILY   Yes.

CHARLOTTE   Has she read any of yours?

EMILY   No.

ANNE   She won't let me.

CHARLOTTE flips through the pages quickly.

Don't rush.

CHARLOTTE flips through a few more pages.

CHARLOTTE   All right.

ANNE   How many did you read?

CHARLOTTE   Enough.

ANNE   Shouldn't you read all of them in order to—

CHARLOTTE   I have a good sense of what they're like.

ANNE   Oh . . . And?

CHARLOTTE   And I find them rather . . . Sweet.

ANNE   Sweet?

CHARLOTTE   There's work to be done on them still—

ANNE   I've been writing these for months.

ANNE grabs her pages back from CHARLOTTE.

CHARLOTTE   Anne . . . They're sincere . . . True.

ANNE   I have more if you want to—

CHARLOTTE   No. No.

Beat.

CHARLOTTE goes to her writing desk and takes out a notebook. In the notebook are several loose pieces of paper. She looks at her sisters, then decides to hand the pages to EMILY. EMILY reads. ANNE rushes over to EMILY and grabs some of the pages out of her hand.

Careful.

ANNE   I want to see.

EMILY   When did you write these?

CHARLOTTE   When I was away . . . In Brussels.

EMILY   I didn't know you were writing . . . Not like this.

CHARLOTTE	I didn't know you were writing either.
EMILY	You have so many. They're strong . . . Stoic.
ANNE	I think there's work to be done on them still.
EMILY	Anne!
ANNE	What?

CHARLOTTE grabs her pages from ANNE.

Charlotte, I didn't mean it like—

CHARLOTTE	It's not that, Anne. It's . . .

CHARLOTTE grabs ANNE's pages too.

How many have you written?

ANNE	Close to twenty.
CHARLOTTE	Emily?
EMILY	I don't know.
CHARLOTTE	You must have some idea.
EMILY	I haven't counted.
CHARLOTTE	How many more could you write? How long would it take?
ANNE	Why?

CHARLOTTE lines the pages side by side on the floor.

CHARLOTTE	Don't you see? What we have?

EMILY and ANNE look at her blankly.

A collection.

ANNE	Of?
CHARLOTTE	Poetry. We can sell these.
ANNE	Sell?
CHARLOTTE	We can sell our work. We can have these published.
ANNE	You want to publish our poems?
CHARLOTTE	Not all of them. But some . . . Yes.
ANNE	You think someone would want to buy what we wrote?
CHARLOTTE	I do.
ANNE	You think our work is strong enough for—
CHARLOTTE	Yes.
ANNE	How would we even go about getting our work published?
CHARLOTTE	We would submit it.
ANNE	To?
CHARLOTTE	To a publisher.
ANNE	We don't know any publishers.

CHARLOTTE	No. But . . . We can review the collections we have. We can submit our work to the same publishers.
ANNE	What if they don't want to publish it?
CHARLOTTE	Then we'll find a publisher that does. We'll send it out until someone finally agrees to—
EMILY	No.

Beat.

Absolutely not.

CHARLOTTE	But what you've written . . . It—
EMILY	It was never meant to be shared.
CHARLOTTE	We've always shared our writing with each other. How many hours have we spent in this very room . . . On this floor . . . Writing away . . . For hours and hours . . . Until there wasn't a drop of ink left in the house? You, me, Anne . . . Bran even. And we would talk . . . Over and over again . . . About publishing our work . . . About publishing our stories.
EMILY	That was when we were children. We didn't know any better.
CHARLOTTE	But what if we did? What if we knew exactly what we—
EMILY	I can't.
CHARLOTTE	Emily.
EMILY	Publish your work if you want. But do it without me. I don't want any part of it.

EMILY heads for the door.

CHARLOTTE   We could make some money.

EMILY stops.

If we sold even a handful of copies—

ANNE   Do writers even make money?

EMILY   It would only be a few pounds . . . If that.

CHARLOTTE   A few pounds will make all the difference. We've used all of Papa's salary for the year already.

EMILY   We haven't had a choice.

ANNE   Because we can't find work.

EMILY   One of you will get a position.

CHARLOTTE   Emily . . . We have been advertising for almost a year.

EMILY   It will change. It has to.

CHARLOTTE   And until then . . . We have this.

Beat.

How many books . . . How many articles, magazines, papers, collections have we read in our lives? We can write just as well as they can. I have the first half of a novel even.

ANNE   I'm writing a novel too. So is she.

EMILY   Anne!

ANNE   You are. I've seen you working on it.

EMILY   That's for me. That's not for—

CHARLOTTE Our work deserves to be published. It deserves to be
           published, translated. It should be read by—

EMILY   Translated?

CHARLOTTE Yes. If our work were published then it would certainly be—

EMILY   Into what language do you want our work translated?

CHARLOTTE In as many languages as possible. French, German—

EMILY   Is that what this is about? You want him to read your work?

CHARLOTTE What? No.

ANNE   Who?

EMILY   This is just another way for you to try and communicate
           with him.

CHARLOTTE Emily.

ANNE   Who are you talking about?

EMILY   Even after he told you . . . Begged you not to. After I told
           you not to—

CHARLOTTE Stop.

ANNE	Why am I always the last one to know anything?
EMILY	This is because of your obsessive—
CHARLOTTE	Stop it.
EMILY	Because of your intolerable . . . unrelenting need to be—
CHARLOTTE	It's because I have absolutely nothing to show for my life!

> *Beat.*

> Every day is exactly the same as the next. We wake up, we eat, we clean, we tend to Papa, we tend to the house, we sew, we read, we write, we sleep. That's it. That's all. Our entire life.

ANNE	We go to church . . . We teach at the school on Sundays.
CHARLOTTE	And we go to church and teach at the school on Sundays, yes.
EMILY	I like our life . . . The life we have.
CHARLOTTE	Because this is the only life you've ever known. You've never wanted more than this. You've barely travelled farther than—
EMILY	I went to school when we were young.
CHARLOTTE	For a few months. Then you got sick . . . Like you always do . . . And came home right away.
EMILY	I went to Brussels with you . . . To study.

CHARLOTTE	For a few months. And then you hurried home as quickly as you could.
EMILY	My life doesn't have any less meaning because I'm satisfied here.
CHARLOTTE	How? How can you be satisfied?
EMILY	I don't crave the sort of attention that you do.
CHARLOTTE	It's not attention I crave. It's a life. I want a life.
EMILY	Go then . . . If you're so miserable. Travel. Or find employment somewhere else. If you want to leave so badly—
CHARLOTTE	I've tried. Every week I advertise that I'm available to work.
	But even if I were hired for a position . . . It's still the same.
	Taking care of other people's children . . . Of other people's homes. Each and every day . . . Wherever we go . . . Wherever we are . . . This life of ours, it's . . .
	Beat.
	How much time do we have left?
ANNE	What?
EMILY	What?
CHARLOTTE	Our entire family . . . Mama, Auntie, our own sisters . . . Everyone we have ever loved has . . .

Beat.

We're lucky to have survived this long. We are. And what do I have to show for it? I have no accomplishments to my name. I'm never going to marry.

ANNE   You think you'll never marry?

CHARLOTTE   I don't see how.

EMILY   You were already proposed to, Charlotte. Twice.

CHARLOTTE   Those didn't count.

EMILY   Yes. They did.

CHARLOTTE   They didn't count for me. Those men didn't know me. They could barely read. I could never have any sort of real love with them. I'll never have that kind of love . . . With anyone.

ANNE   You don't know that.

CHARLOTTE   I do. If those men were my best chance at marriage then . . . It's better to accept it and look forward. It isn't wise for a woman without any sort of beauty or fortune to—

ANNE   You have beauty.

CHARLOTTE   Where?

ANNE   You have beauty in you.

EMILY   Charlotte . . . You're beautiful.

CHARLOTTE   No.

EMILY   To us you are.

CHARLOTTE   And to everyone else? I know what I am. A woman like me
                 shouldn't make marriage the basis for her hopes and wishes.
                 The two of you still have a chance at marriage.

ANNE   Us?

CHARLOTTE   Why not. You're young.

EMILY   We're not that young.

CHARLOTTE   You're young enough.

ANNE   I won't marry . . . Never. Not after losing—

CHARLOTTE   Anne . . . You were never going to marry him.

ANNE   Yes.

CHARLOTTE   It was nothing more than a flirtation. There was no talk of
                 marriage. He didn't talk to Papa about marrying—

ANNE   He intended to. If he hadn't passed away—

CHARLOTTE   Anne—

ANNE   If he hadn't passed we would be together this very
                 moment . . . In a house of our own . . . With a family.

                 Beat.

I was absolutely going to marry him, Charlotte. You know that.

ANNE stands, then plops herself down in the rocking chair.

Beat.

CHARLOTTE begins to tidy the papers.

That's it?

CHARLOTTE   I suppose so.

CHARLOTTE looks at EMILY.

EMILY   Whatever you think will come of this . . . It may have no effect whatsoever on our lives . . . Nothing may change. And then what?

CHARLOTTE   Then I see no harm in trying.

EMILY   You have your work . . . Anne's work. You have more than enough to create something between the two of you.

CHARLOTTE   We can't move forward without you.

ANNE   If she doesn't want to be a part of it there's no point in forcing her.

EMILY   Do you . . . Want to be a part of it? Want to publish your—

ANNE   Yes. I've always wanted this.

EMILY   You'd have a better chance if I'm nowhere near it.

CHARLOTTE   That's not true.

EMILY   It is.

CHARLOTTE   We need your work.

EMILY   If you're in such dire need of a third, ask Branwell. He's the one with the talent.

CHARLOTTE   Oh, Emily! How can you not see it? You have a gift. Do you know how many people spend their lives searching for what you have?

EMILY   What I write is . . . Strange. It's not suitable . . . Or dignified. It in no way reflects how a woman should feel . . . Or think . . . Or write. I know that. No one will understand it. No one will want to—

CHARLOTTE   If you were a man, do you think for a moment you would choose not to pursue—

EMILY   If I were a man I wouldn't have to choose.

ANNE   Then just pretend you're a man and be done with it.

EMILY   I can't pretend to be something I'm not.

ANNE   Why not?

EMILY   Because it . . . It's not—

ANNE   Because it's not what?

CHARLOTTE   You can. You can.

CHARLOTTE stands, grabs paper and a quill, and writes.

We could keep our initials . . . Keep the first letters for each of our names. The rest can be whatever we like . . .

CHARLOTTE holds the page up for them to see.

ANNE   Currer, Ellis, Aaron Bell?

CHARLOTTE   If they think we're men they'll focus on what we write . . . Not who we are. We can send our work out without being afraid of anyone knowing. We can write what we like . . . How we like.

ANNE grabs the page from CHARLOTTE.

ANNE   Why Bell? Why can't we use our last name?

CHARLOTTE   People know there's only one son in our family.

ANNE   How many people know that?

CHARLOTTE   Enough.

ANNE   Can't we submit anonymously?

CHARLOTTE   No. Our work could be stolen. And we would have no way to prove it was ours.

EMILY   Work with a name is respected far more than anything written anonymously.

ANNE   Currer, Ellis, Aaron. Mine doesn't sound nearly as intriguing as yours. Aaron . . . It's so plain.

CHARLOTTE   What then?

ANNE   Adam, Abram, Andrew, Arthur, Alfred—

EMILY   Acton.

ANNE   Oh . . . Acton! Yes! Currer, Ellis, Acton Bell.

CHARLOTTE writes the names out again. She holds it up for them to see.

So . . . No one would know it was us?

CHARLOTTE   No one would know it was us.

ANNE   What about Papa? We would have to tell him.

CHARLOTTE   Papa would go mad knowing we were trying to be published. He would get too invested. He would want to change everything we wrote.

EMILY   He would edit every poem until he was satisfied.

CHARLOTTE   Until he felt it was up to his standards.

EMILY   And if it weren't a resounding success . . . He would never forgive us.

CHARLOTTE   No. We don't tell him. We don't tell Branwell. It stays between the three of us.

ANNE   Then . . . What's the point?

EMILY   I won't do it if we tell people . . . That's the point.

CHARLOTTE	But if we don't tell people? Then you'll . . .

EMILY looks at the page with their proposed names on it.

EMILY	We shouldn't have to disguise who we are.
CHARLOTTE	Oh, Emily! Does it really matter? It would be a few published copies of a poetry collection. That's it. That's all it is.
EMILY	I don't know.
CHARLOTTE	Emily! Can't you at least try to—
ANNE	Just say yes, Emily! For goodness' sake!

EMILY looks at her sisters, and exhales heavily.

INTERLUDE

CHARLOTTE, EMILY, and ANNE *grab small stacks of blank pages and quills. They sit at the table and write. As they do, they hand each other their pages. They read one another's work. They make notes. They hand the pages back to the author. They sit and write.*

Again, they hand each other their pages. They read one another's work, make notes, and hand the pages back to each other. They sit. They write.

Again, they hand each other their pages. They read one another's work and make notes. They start to form a pile in the middle of the table.

The stack of paper grows. These are the pages of their poetry collection.

CHARLOTTE *gently picks up the pages and leaves the room.*

EMILY *and* ANNE *grab another small stack of blank pages. Again they start to write. They share their work with each other. They each begin a stack of their own.*

CHARLOTTE enters with a small book in hand—a printed copy of their poetry collection. EMILY and ANNE gather beside CHARLOTTE. They look at it together, smile, place it on their bookshelf, and get back to work.

CHARLOTTE grabs another small stack of blank pages. They write. They share their work with each other. The stack of paper grows. These are the pages of their novels.

CHARLOTTE collects the pages from EMILY and ANNE. Together they tie the piles with twine, fold an envelope out of a large sheet of paper, and seal it shut. CHARLOTTE takes the envelope and leaves.

MOVEMENT 3

Afternoon. Nine months later.

The front door of the house is opened, then closed quickly.

ANNE, twenty-seven, enters the room, out of breath. She wears a day dress, bonnet, and shawl. She takes out a large envelope she was hiding under her shawl and places it on the sofa. She places the shawl on the envelope to hide it. Then she leaves the room.

Beat.

EMILY, twenty-eight, enters with a book and teacup. She sits and reads. She wears a housedress.

ANNE *(calling to them)* Charlotte? Emily?

EMILY *(calling back)* I'm here.

ANNE *(calling back)* Charlotte? Emily?

EMILY *(calling back)* What? I'm in here.

ANNE runs back into the room, breathing heavily.

Why are you so out of breath?

ANNE   I ran.

EMILY   The whole way?

ANNE   Yes.

EMILY   Anne . . . You shouldn't have.

ANNE   It doesn't matter.

          EMILY hands ANNE her teacup.

EMILY   Here.

          ANNE drinks quickly.

ANNE   Owww.

EMILY   It's hot.

ANNE   You could have told me that before I drank—

EMILY   I thought you could feel how hot it was when you picked
              up the—

ANNE   My tongue.

          EMILY takes the cup from ANNE and blows on the tea.

              Charlotte . . . Where is she?

EMILY   She went to town.

ANNE   She should have come with me. I would have waited for her. Why didn't she come?

EMILY hands the cup back to ANNE.

EMILY   Drink it slowly.

ANNE takes a sip.

ANNE   Where's Papa?

EMILY   At the church.

ANNE   And Bran?

EMILY   Asleep. If you didn't wake him with your shouting.

EMILY notices ANNE's shawl on the sofa.

Hang it up.

ANNE   I will.

EMILY   Now. If you don't hang it up you'll forget all about it and then Charlotte will come home and make a big—

ANNE goes to the sofa. She pulls out the envelope and holds it up for EMILY to see.

It's . . .

ANNE   Yes.

EMILY takes the envelope and feels it.

EMILY	It's . . . Lighter.

ANNE	I know.

EMILY	Thinner.

ANNE	I know.

They look at each other. EMILY places the envelope on the table.

EMILY	We'll open it when Charlotte returns.

ANNE	When will that be?

EMILY	I don't know . . . A couple of hours.

ANNE	A couple of hours? I had to carry that all the way here . . . Unopened . . . And even that took all my strength. Now you want me to wait a couple of hours? I should have opened it the moment I saw it.

EMILY	No. You were right to wait until we were all together.

ANNE	I can't wait for her.

EMILY	Anne.

ANNE moves to grab the envelope. EMILY grabs it before she can get to it.

We're going to wait.

ANNE	I can't.

ANNE lunges at EMILY. EMILY moves out of the way.

EMILY   Stop it. Be patient.

ANNE   Can't we just open it?

EMILY   No.

ANNE   She won't even know.

EMILY   Yes. She will.

ANNE   What if we open it . . . Wrap it back up again . . . And make
             it look exactly like it did before we opened it? How would
             she know then?

EMILY   Because . . . You're a terrible liar.

ANNE   I can lie.

EMILY   Not very well.

ANNE   Neither can you.

EMILY   Which is why we're going to wait.

ANNE   Why did we agree to this?

EMILY   You were the one who insisted.

ANNE   No.

EMILY   Yes. You insisted that if we received any sort of correspon-
             dence about our work we'd open it together.

ANNE	Well . . . If I proposed the idea can't I be the one to change it?
EMILY	No. We submitted our novels together . . . We open the responses together.
ANNE	This is more painful than waiting to hear about our poetry collection.

EMILY puts the envelope on the table.

EMILY	Leave it.

EMILY goes back to her book.

ANNE	Now what I am supposed to do?
EMILY	Try . . . Sitting.

ANNE sits in the rocking chair. She looks at the envelope.

Why don't you do something while you sit?

ANNE	I can't do anything.
EMILY	Try.

ANNE grabs a book. She flips through the pages, never taking her eyes off the envelope. She flips through the book faster and faster until finally . . .

ANNE	I can't!

ANNE drops her book and heads for the table. EMILY makes it to the envelope before ANNE does.

Give it to me.

ANNE chases EMILY around the table.

EMILY   You shouldn't run.

ANNE   I don't care. Give it to me.

EMILY   Anne!

ANNE   Give it!

ANNE tries to grab the envelope from EMILY. EMILY sticks the envelope up her skirt and holds it between her legs.

You think that's going to stop me?

EMILY   I should hope so.

Beat.

ANNE chases after EMILY. EMILY takes the envelope out from her skirt and runs. She drops the envelope on the floor. ANNE nearly grabs it, but EMILY picks it up before she can.

ANNE   Emily!

EMILY   Anne!

ANNE   Please! Every other envelope had all three novels sent back to us. This one is thinner. What does that mean?

EMILY   It can mean all sorts of things. A publisher spilled on one of the manuscripts. They destroyed it and—

ANNE	Destroyed? Those are our only copies.
EMILY	We won't know until we—
ANNE	Charlotte would have opened it already. You know she would have. If she saw how much thinner it was . . . She would have opened it without a moment's hesitation.
EMILY	Well . . . We're not Charlotte.
ANNE	What if it's a positive response? She wouldn't be upset with us for opening it if it's a positive response.
EMILY	And if it isn't?
ANNE	Then . . . She'll be so distracted by her grief that she'll forget that we opened it in the first place.

EMILY places the envelope on the table. ANNE moves toward her.

EMILY	Don't.

ANNE backs away.

ANNE	This is painful.

They hear stumbling in the hallway. They look at each other. EMILY and ANNE go to the door.

	I thought Papa was going to watch him today.
EMILY	Papa was called to church.
ANNE	He couldn't have taken Bran with him?

EMILY	No.
ANNE	I don't like being alone in the house with him.
EMILY	He's been quiet today. I've hardly seen him.
ANNE	What? No fit of despair?
EMILY	No. Not yet.

They hear the front door to the house open then close.
EMILY and ANNE go to the window.

ANNE	Now where is he going?
EMILY	You know where he's going. To a pub.
ANNE	Which pub?
EMILY	Whichever one will still serve him.
ANNE	Did you hear the way he yelled at Papa . . . when he refused to give him more money? Papa . . . of all people.
EMILY	When a man wants to drink . . . he'll stop at nothing.
ANNE	Emily . . . what would have happened? If you hadn't been here when he—
EMILY	It's best not to think about it.
ANNE	I can't help it. What if something awful happened to Bran . . . To you?
EMILY	It didn't.

ANNE	But it could have. You could have been burnt . . . Or worse.
EMILY	I wasn't. We got out of the house in time.
ANNE	Still . . . What was he thinking? Lighting his bed on fire? How cruel does one have to be to do something so—
EMILY	Anne . . . He was trying to take his own life.
ANNE	Don't. Don't say that.
EMILY	When I found him in his room . . . He was on the floor. He fainted from the smoke. I bent down to lift him up. When he came to . . . He begged me to leave him there . . . Alone. He begged me to—
ANNE	He has no right to put us through this . . . To put Papa through—
EMILY	He has nothing left to live for.
ANNE	He has plenty to live for.
EMILY	He feels as if he has nothing to—
ANNE	Why? Because she finally wrote to say they were never going to be together?
EMILY	Yes. When her husband died, Bran started to believe that . . . That perhaps they would marry after all.
ANNE	She was never going to marry him.

Beat.

	Why did Charlotte go to town?
EMILY	I'm not sure.
ANNE	Yes you are.
EMILY	If she wants you to know she'll tell you herself.
ANNE	No she won't. Is she all right?
EMILY	She's . . . Fine.
ANNE	Then why can't you tell me why she—
EMILY	It's not my business to tell.
ANNE	She tells you everything.
EMILY	She doesn't tell me—
ANNE	Charlotte tells you everything and the two of you never bother to include me or ask me or even think to—
EMILY	She's seeing the doctor about her eyes. Her sight . . . It's getting worse.
ANNE	Are her eyes as bad as Papa's were?
EMILY	She doesn't know.
ANNE	It took us over a year to save enough for him to have his surgery. And we still had to use our inheritance. We can't afford for her to have the same procedure. We've already sold everything we could. We can't—

EMILY	She doesn't know. Don't say anything to her. She's so sensitive about these sorts of things.
ANNE	She's sensitive about everything.

    Beat.

What if they said no?

EMILY	Then Charlotte will send it the next publisher on the list.
ANNE	And when we reach the end of the list? Then what?

    ANNE picks up the envelope.

It isn't right.

    EMILY shoots her a look. ANNE drops the envelope, as if surrendering.

The fact that she's using the same envelope every time she sends our novels out? She shouldn't be crossing out their names like this.

EMILY	It's just an envelope.
ANNE	Emily . . . These sorts of things mean something. Any time our package is sent to a publisher they can see who else has rejected us. We should have used a new envelope every time we—
EMILY	We can't afford a new envelope every time we—
ANNE	Don't you think that if someone saw the number of names crossed out it would alter the perception of our work? If

I saw that six other publishers had already rejected these novels—

EMILY   That may have had no impact on the responses we've received so far.

ANNE   Then why has no one wanted to publish our novels yet?

EMILY   I . . . I don't know.

   Beat.

ANNE   The same publisher that published our poems should be the one to—

EMILY   They don't publish novels.

ANNE   Well . . . They should. They were pleased with how our collection was received. Why wouldn't they consider—

EMILY   They weren't pleased.

ANNE   Yes.

EMILY   Anne, we only sold two copies out of a thousand.

ANNE   Two is better than nothing. And the reviews were positive . . . Yours especially. You received more praise than Charlotte and I combined.

EMILY   We were reviewed by three people.

ANNE   Well . . . It wasn't a good year for poetry.

EMILY   It's never a good year for poetry.

Beat.

ANNE   Do you think it's mine? It felt about the weight of mine.

EMILY   You don't know how much your novel weighs.

ANNE   It isn't much thicker than that.

EMILY   Neither is mine.

EMILY picks up the envelope to feel the weight of it.

This isn't yours.

ANNE   It could be. The title of my novel alone—

EMILY   You have a fine title.

ANNE   Not as fine as yours. *Wuthering Heights* has such—

EMILY   It's only a title.

ANNE   Titles mean everything. *Agnes Grey* . . . It's dull.

EMILY   It's the name of your main character. Many, many titles are the name of the main character.

ANNE   It's too simple.

EMILY   Charlotte's title is just as simple. *The Professor?* That's not commanding or—

ANNE   My novel is the weakest of the three.

EMILY   You can't think like that.

ANNE	What if I'm not a writer?
EMILY	Anne . . . Do you write?
ANNE	Yes.
EMILY	Then you're a writer. You spend more time writing than either Charlotte or I do.
ANNE	Only in an attempt to be as good as you.
EMILY	Anne . . . You are good.
ANNE	But I don't want to be good. I want to be great.
EMILY	You are great.
ANNE	You said good.
EMILY	Anne . . . It doesn't mean—
ANNE	It means everything! To me . . . It means . . .

Beat.

What if I'm never . . . It's torture.

EMILY	It's torture for all of us.
ANNE	Not for you. Every time we receive a rejection you seem fine . . . Relieved even. Doesn't it hurt to know that someone doesn't want to publish your work?
EMILY	Yes. It's unbearable. It's agony.

ANNE   You don't show it.

EMILY   Maybe I'm a better liar than you think.

            Beat.

ANNE   What if it never happens for us?

            *They look at each other. ANNE pulls a letter from her
            pocket and hands it to EMILY to read.*

            They have three children. All girls. All under the age of five.
            They would need me for a few years . . . At least. They want
            me to start in a month.

EMILY   When did you get this?

ANNE   Today. It arrived with the envelope.

EMILY   This is the first response you've received in . . . In over a year.

ANNE   I know.

EMILY   Are you going to write to them?

ANNE   Should I?

EMILY   I didn't know you were still advertising for a position.
            Charlotte gave up months ago.

ANNE   I kept posting. Just in case.

EMILY   Anne. Oh, Anne.

ANNE   Emily . . .

Beat.

If it's mine . . . If my novel is the one they . . . I can't keep going on like this. It might be time for me to just . . . To be sent this letter on the same day we received another rejection.

EMILY   We don't know what's in there.

ANNE   One of our novels is in there.

EMILY   And it might very well be mine.

ANNE   It won't be.

EMILY   We won't know until we—

ANNE   Every time we're rejected . . . I wonder if it's me that's holding us back. If we had submitted our novels separately yours would already have been published.

EMILY   That's not true.

ANNE   Yes.

EMILY   Anne.

ANNE   I want to be like you . . . Like Charlotte. I want it so badly . . . Sometimes I can't stand to look at you . . . Or be in the same room as you. Every time our work is rejected I torment myself thinking that if only I were as good as you—

EMILY   You are.

ANNE   It's too much. All of this. It's too—

EMILY   You can't give up.

ANNE   I have to. I can't . . .

            The front door of the house is opened then closed
            quickly. EMILY *and* ANNE *look at each other.*

            CHARLOTTE, *thirty-one, opens the door. She wears a day*
            dress. She immediately sees ANNE's *shawl on the sofa.*

CHARLOTTE   Put it away.

EMILY   Never mind the—

CHARLOTTE   Anne. Put it away.

            ANNE *holds up the envelope for* CHARLOTTE *to see.*

            It's . . . thinner.

ANNE   Yes.

CHARLOTTE   You didn't open it?

ANNE   Emily wouldn't let me.

EMILY   We were waiting for you.

CHARLOTTE   You should have opened it.

ANNE   I told you!

EMILY   We agreed to open them together.

ANNE   Open it . . . Open it this very moment.

| CHARLOTTE | It's so thin. What does it mean? |
| ANNE | It means we need to open it. |

CHARLOTTE hands the envelope to EMILY.

CHARLOTTE	You.
EMILY	Me?
ANNE	Emily! Open it!

Beat.

EMILY opens the envelope. She takes out a letter and reads to herself.

What?

EMILY reads.

What does it say?

Beat.

CHARLOTTE	Emily? What does it—
EMILY	No.
ANNE	No as in . . .
EMILY	As in they've declined to publish our novels.
CHARLOTTE	All of them?

EMILY   Yes.

CHARLOTTE   That can't be.

> *CHARLOTTE moves toward EMILY. EMILY grabs the contents of the envelope before CHARLOTTE can get to it.*

ANNE   What did they send back?

EMILY   It doesn't matter.

CHARLOTTE   What did they send in the envelope?

ANNE   Read us the letter.

EMILY   I told you what it says.

ANNE   I want to hear it.

CHARLOTTE   What did they send?

> *Beat.*

> *ANNE rushes to EMILY and tries to grab the envelope from her.*

ANNE   Give it to me.

EMILY   Enough.

ANNE   I have to know this very moment.

EMILY   Stop. You're acting like a child.

CHARLOTTE   Emily. Give it to her.

ANNE tries to wrestle the letter away from EMILY. EMILY pushes ANNE away and rips the letter into little pieces.

ANNE   No!

                ANNE runs to pick the pieces of the letter up off the floor.

                Why would you do that?

CHARLOTTE   What's come over you?

EMILY   You wouldn't listen.

                CHARLOTTE looks at EMILY.

CHARLOTTE   Give it to me.

EMILY   No.

CHARLOTTE   We have every right to see.

                CHARLOTTE follows EMILY.

EMILY   Enough.

CHARLOTTE   Hold her.

EMILY   Don't touch me.

                ANNE holds EMILY from behind. CHARLOTTE tries to wrestle the package away from EMILY. They struggle. It brings them to the floor. EMILY bites CHARLOTTE's hand.

CHARLOTTE   Owww. You broke skin.

EMILY   Satisfied?

CHARLOTTE   No.

               CHARLOTTE lunges at EMILY. EMILY moves away. ANNE
               grabs the envelope out of her hands.

ANNE   Ha!

CHARLOTTE   Give it here.

ANNE   No!

CHARLOTTE   Anne. Give it to me or I swear I'll—

ANNE   All right. All right.

               ANNE hands the envelope to CHARLOTTE. CHARLOTTE
               opens it.

               What? What is it?

               CHARLOTTE reads.

EMILY   Charlotte . . .

               CHARLOTTE reads.

               Charlotte.

               CHARLOTTE looks at EMILY.

               Beat.

CHARLOTTE *hurls the package on the floor. She throws the door open and runs out of the room.*

ANNE *looks at the pages on the floor.*

ANNE   They sent back ... Hers? *The Professor?* They want to publish ours? Yours ... And mine?

Beat.

ANNE *heads for the door.*

EMILY   Don't.

ANNE   We should go to her. She shouldn't be—

EMILY   Anne ... Leave her. She needs time to—

The slamming of a door can be heard from upstairs.

Beat.

EMILY *and* ANNE *look at each other.*

INTERLUDE

EMILY and ANNE tidy the room. Books are added back to the shelf. New cushions replace older ones on the sofa. New quills replace older ones on the table.

CHARLOTTE enters with a stack of blank pages. She sits at one end of the table and writes ferociously. As she completes a page she creates a stack in front of her. She is writing her next novel.

When her stack is large enough CHARLOTTE grabs her pages and leaves.

EMILY and ANNE watch her, then leave.

CHARLOTTE enters with a book in hand—a printed copy of her novel. CHARLOTTE places it on the bookshelf. She reaches for a stack of newspapers. She sits at the table and reads.

MOVEMENT 4

Evening. Fourteen months later.

CHARLOTTE, thirty-two, sits at the table reading from the stack of newspapers. She is dressed for bed.

EMILY   *(calling from off stage)* Charlotte!

CHARLOTTE starts to tidy the papers on the table.

(calling from off stage) Charlotte!

CHARLOTTE   *(calling back)* Coming.

CHARLOTTE finishes with the papers then leaves the room.

EMILY, thirty, enters. She is dressed for bed. She goes to the bookshelf and grabs a Bible. As she heads for the door, she stops. She takes a moment for herself and sits at the table. She notices the stack of newspapers and starts to read them.

ANNE, twenty-eight, peeks her head into the room. She is carrying a basin and cloth. She is also dressed for bed.

EMILY tidies the newspapers.

ANNE　　　　　What are those?

EMILY　　　　　Nothing. Here.

　　　　　　　　EMILY hands ANNE the Bible.

　　　　　　　　Take this to Papa.

　　　　　　　　EMILY has a tickle in her throat and coughs.

ANNE　　　　　What are you doing with those?

EMILY　　　　　Go. Papa needs it.

ANNE　　　　　Bran's been refusing for weeks to let Papa bless him.

EMILY　　　　　Well . . . He's finally agreed.

ANNE　　　　　A lot of good it will do him now.

EMILY　　　　　It might. Three days ago he was strong enough to be in town.

ANNE　　　　　He's fading. Charlotte can't even look at him. He keeps reaching his hand out to touch her from bed. She just stands in the doorway . . . Staring back at him.

　　　　　　　　Beat.

　　　　　　　　I think we should tell him . . . Bran.

EMILY　　　　　Tell him what?

ANNE　　　　　About our work . . . About our novels.

EMILY	Why?
ANNE	I don't want him to pass without knowing.
EMILY	It's too early to know if he's going to pass or not.
ANNE	He's fading.

CHARLOTTE enters the room. She covers her mouth.

CHARLOTTE	The air in that room . . . We shouldn't be in there.
ANNE	We can't leave Papa alone with him.
CHARLOTTE	We could catch it.
ANNE	So could Papa.
EMILY	The doctor said it might only be a cold.
ANNE	You don't cough up blood with a cold.
CHARLOTTE	Whatever it is . . . We shouldn't be in there.
ANNE	Charlotte . . .
CHARLOTTE	What?
EMILY	Nothing. We were going up.

EMILY goes to leave.

ANNE	I want to tell him.
EMILY	Anne!

ANNE	I do. I want to tell Bran about our work.
EMILY	Now's not the time to decide that.
ANNE	Now's exactly the time. If he passes tonight—
EMILY	He might not pass.
ANNE	But if he does . . . Then we'll have kept this entire thing from him.

He should know. |
EMILY	Why?
ANNE	He's our brother. I don't want secrets between us in what might be his final hours.
EMILY	Because he hasn't kept secrets from us?
ANNE	I don't care. I want him to know.
CHARLOTTE	So do I.
EMILY	Both of you?
CHARLOTTE	Yes. Why wouldn't we tell him?
EMILY	We agreed that we wouldn't say anything . . . to anyone about what we've done . . . Under any circumstances.
ANNE	It's just Bran. Who would he tell? He's not seeing any visitors.
EMILY	Anne, no one is supposed to know.

ANNE   But think of how it would make him feel to learn about
                what we—

EMILY   Bran is in no state to . . . He can't see straight . . . He can't
                think straight . . . He can't tell the three of us apart. Now
                is not the time to—

CHARLOTTE   It would bring him comfort. Papa was reading to him earlier
                tonight. Imagine reading to him from one of our novels.

EMILY   You can't stand to be in the same room as Bran. Now you
                want to remind him of all the things he hasn't done with
                his life?

CHARLOTTE   No. Sharing our work with him . . . with Papa would—

EMILY   With . . . Papa? You want to tell—

CHARLOTTE   If we're telling Bran . . . We have to tell Papa.

                EMILY looks at CHARLOTTE and ANNE.

EMILY   You've talked about this?

ANNE   No.

EMILY   You've spoken about this without me?

ANNE   No. Emily. It was only an idea.

EMILY   How long have you had this idea for?

ANNE   Not long. But seeing him in bed. With no colour in his
                cheeks. He looks so thin—

EMILY	And you?
CHARLOTTE	What?
EMILY	How long have you wanted to tell Bran? Tell Papa about our—
CHARLOTTE	Emily . . . You're overreacting.
EMILY	How long?
CHARLOTTE	What does it matter?
EMILY	I want to know why you're breaking a promise that we made—
CHARLOTTE	I'm not breaking a promise. If I were, I would have told them already.
EMILY	But you want to.
CHARLOTTE	Yes. Emily. I want my own father and brother to know what we've done . . . What we've achieved. Did you honestly think we would never tell anyone?
EMILY	Yes, Charlotte. That was the only reason I ever agreed to—
CHARLOTTE	And if we've changed our minds? The two of us shouldn't be punished for wanting them to know.
EMILY	No one is punishing you, Charlotte.
CHARLOTTE	You are. By having a fit at even the thought of—
EMILY	Do you have any idea what it's—

EMILY lunges toward CHARLOTTE. ANNE stops her.

ANNE   Emily. Don't.

EMILY   Do you not see what it's been like . . . For us?

ANNE   We should go upstairs.

EMILY   Why we might not want Papa . . . Or Bran to know?

CHARLOTTE   Papa would be proud. They both would be.

EMILY   They would be proud of you, Charlotte. You're the one being sent letters of praise from readers . . . From other authors. You're the one invited to make appearances. You're the one receiving glowing reviews. But we . . .

ANNE   Tonight is not the night to—

EMILY   Do you have any idea how dreadful these past few months have been?

CHARLOTTE   Your novel received positive reviews, Emily.

EMILY   One . . . One positive review. The rest were completely—

CHARLOTTE   There will be more. It takes time for these things to—

EMILY   It didn't take any time for you. The moment *Jane Eyre* was published . . . The moment it was released—

CHARLOTTE   You may still receive the same sort of—

EMILY   I won't. We won't. You know that.

CHARLOTTE   I don't know that, Emily. All I can do is hope the two of
               you have the same sort of—

               *EMILY goes to the table. She grabs the newspapers and
               drops them in front of CHARLOTTE.*

EMILY   Why would you bring these here?

               Beat.

               Charlotte . . . Why would you—

CHARLOTTE   I asked for the latest round of reviews to be sent to me.

EMILY   The three of us agreed not to have any more reviews in the
               house.

CHARLOTTE   You weren't supposed to read them.

EMILY   You left them here . . . Out in the open. Why wouldn't you
               take them to your room if you didn't want—

CHARLOTTE   I didn't have time to put them away. And I certainly didn't
               leave them out for you to find.

EMILY   Have you read them?

               Beat.

               Charlotte . . .

               Beat.

               Have you or have you not read them—

CHARLOTTE	I glanced at them.
EMILY	Glanced?
CHARLOTTE	Yes.
EMILY	Sit.
CHARLOTTE	Emily. This isn't—
EMILY	Sit!

CHARLOTTE sits. EMILY coughs.

ANNE	Emily.

EMILY looks through the pile of newspaper clippings.

EMILY	"Heathcliff, as depicted by the deranged Ellis Bell, is a deformed monster. This is a bad novel. A bad novel indeed."

EMILY picks up another review.

"If this book is the first work of the author we hope that he doesn't produce a second or a third novel. We hope, both for his sake and ours, that he never attempts at writing another novel again."

EMILY picks up another review.

"We come from the reading of *Wuthering Heights* as if we had come fresh from a pest-house. Read *Jane Eyre*. Burn *Wuthering Heights*."

CHARLOTTE chuckles.

This is amusing to you?

CHARLOTTE   You can't take those seriously . . . Most of them are so poorly
written. You can't take it to heart.

EMILY   How can I not when I have put all of my heart into it?
They've destroyed the very thing that I've—

CHARLOTTE   It hasn't been destroyed.

EMILY   Burn *Wuthering Heights*?

CHARLOTTE   You have to have a thicker skin if you're going to continue.

EMILY   I can't. I can't continue.

ANNE   Emily, you have to.

EMILY   Why? So I can be humiliated again and again? I would have
never done any of this if it hadn't been for you.

CHARLOTTE   Yes. You were perfectly prepared to spend the rest of your
life wasting your time . . . Your talent—

EMILY   You're the only ones who seem to think I have any talent.

CHARLOTTE   It was your first attempt. A first novel is difficult. So much
of what you wrote is commendable. But there was . . .

EMILY   What? There was what?

CHARLOTTE   I told you there would be no sympathy for Heathcliff. I told
you not to depict him as such a—

EMILY   Such a what?

CHARLOTTE   As such a beast. I warned you. I gave you my thoughts.

EMILY   Your thoughts were to change everything I'd written.

CHARLOTTE   I told you to make some adjustments.

EMILY   And if only I had listened to you then none of this would have happened. Is that it?

CHARLOTTE   You might have been more satisfied with what you wrote if you—

EMILY   I was.

EMILY coughs.

I was satisfied!

CHARLOTTE   Emily!

EMILY coughs.

ANNE   Enough. Both of you.

ANNE goes to the papers and collects them. As she does, she reads.

CHARLOTTE   She's the one making this harder for herself.

EMILY   You're the one that—

EMILY coughs.

CHARLOTTE   It's a privilege to have your work reviewed at all. To have created something worthy of—

ANNE	These are terrible.
EMILY	Thank you, Anne. They're utterly and completely—
ANNE	There's hardly any mention of me in any of these. "And *Agnes Grey*, written by the lacklustre Acton Bell, leaves no impression at all." That's it. That's all there is. They're all about Emily. We published our novels together. Why wouldn't they write as much about my work as they did about hers?
EMILY	I'd rather leave no impression than be considered deranged or—
ANNE	I wouldn't. I want them to talk about me . . . About my work.
EMILY	And if they're saying monstrous things?
ANNE	That's better than being forgotten . . . Or compared to you.
EMILY	Well, they compare me to her so . . .
CHARLOTTE	And they compare me to everyone else. It doesn't matter what they say.
EMILY	You can only say that because the reviews you got—
CHARLOTTE	Not every review I got was positive.
EMILY / ANNE	Yes!
ANNE	Almost every single one you got was—
EMILY	If your work received an ounce of the criticism mine has, we'd be spending weeks picking you up off this very floor.

EMILY coughs.

I know why you want Papa and Bran to . . . But for me . . . For us. If Papa knew how poorly it had been received—

CHARLOTTE   You don't think that Papa might form his own opinions about your work?

EMILY   I don't want him to have any opinions about it at all.

EMILY coughs.

ANNE   Should I get some tea?

EMILY shakes her head.

CHARLOTTE   Are you sure?

EMILY   Yes.

EMILY clears her throat.

CHARLOTTE   People need to know what we've done. There's already too much confusion around the entire—

EMILY   What confusion?

CHARLOTTE goes to her writing desk and takes out a letter.

CHARLOTTE   Your idiotic publisher has been claiming that *Jane Eyre* and *Agnes Grey* were written by the same author . . . by the same man.

ANNE   What?

ANNE grabs the letter out of CHARLOTTE's hand.

They think you wrote *Agnes Grey*?

CHARLOTTE   They're saying that I wrote—

ANNE   But . . . You didn't. You didn't write my—

CHARLOTTE   I am perfectly aware that I didn't write your novel, Anne. I'm not saying I did. But your publisher is. And now my publisher is furious. This has gone on long enough. People need to know the truth.

EMILY   What truth?

CHARLOTTE   That we're women. That there are three of us. That we're sisters. And that we've each written our own novels.

ANNE   Yes. This needs to be resolved right away. I don't want this hanging over our heads when I publish my next book.

EMILY   Your next . . . What?

ANNE   I've been writing a second novel.

CHARLOTTE   So have I.

EMILY   You . . . Have?

ANNE   We should go in person. To prove we are who we say we are.

CHARLOTTE   Yes. All three of us should go.

EMILY   This was never part of the plan. It was never—

They hear a noise above them.

Beat.

They hear their father sobbing. They look at each other, silently negotiating who should go upstairs. Finally . . .

ANNE   I'll go.

ANNE grabs the Bible and leaves.

CHARLOTTE   Emily . . .

Beat.

EMILY   It's changing . . . Changed.

CHARLOTTE   What?

EMILY   My life . . . Our lives.

CHARLOTTE sits near EMILY.

CHARLOTTE   Can you not be happy for me?

EMILY   I am. Of course I am.

CHARLOTTE   Then?

Beat.

EMILY   You've outdone us.

EMILY lays her head in CHARLOTTE's lap.

Beat.

ANNE enters.

CHARLOTTE   What?

ANNE   He's gone.

EMILY   What?

ANNE   Bran . . . He . . .

> *Beat.*

> *They look at each other.*

Papa is asking for you.

EMILY   I can go.

ANNE   He asked for Charlotte.

> *CHARLOTTE goes to the door. She looks back at her sisters and leaves.*

> *Beat.*

> *EMILY clears her throat. She starts to cough.*

Emily?

> *EMILY coughs to the point of not being able to stand up straight.*

Emily!

ANNE goes to EMILY. EMILY covers her mouth with a cloth. When she pulls it away she reveals blood.

No. No, no, no, no, no.

EMILY's coughing becomes uncontrollable. ANNE tries to comfort her.

(calling out) Charlotte!

EMILY coughs. ANNE holds EMILY tightly.

(calling out) Charlotte!

INTERLUDE

ANNE tries to pick EMILY up, but struggles. CHARLOTTE enters. Together they lead EMILY out of the room.

The room is empty for a moment.

CHARLOTTE enters. She carries a few crates filled with books. She puts the crate on the table, then leaves the room.

ANNE enters. She also carries a crate filled with books. She puts her crate on the table, then leaves the room.

CHARLOTTE enters again and begins to organize the room.

ANNE enters. She carries a tray with a teapot and two teacups on it. She puts it on the table.

ANNE sits in the rocking chair and begins to sew. CHARLOTTE continues to organize the room.

MOVEMENT 5

Evening. Four months later.

CHARLOTTE, thirty-two, organizes books on the bookshelf. She wears glasses now. ANNE, twenty-eight, sits in her rocking chair with her shawl wrapped around her. She repairs a skirt.

They are both dressed for bed.

ANNE stands to pour some tea. She moves slowly. She hands CHARLOTTE a cup. CHARLOTTE takes a sip and makes a face.

CHARLOTTE   It's strong.

ANNE   Do you want me to make you another?

CHARLOTTE   No. No. It's fine.

ANNE takes her cup and sips. She sits in the rocking chair. She has a tickle in her throat. She tries to clear it. CHARLOTTE watches ANNE closely.

You don't have to do that. I can buy a new one.

ANNE	I'm almost done.

CHARLOTTE puts some books on the shelf.

Why don't you finish that tomorrow?

CHARLOTTE	I want to finish tonight.

CHARLOTTE moves some books and accidentally knocks them over.

ANNE	I thought your glasses are supposed to help.
CHARLOTTE	They are helping.

CHARLOTTE collects the books off the floor. ANNE stands to help her.

Anne . . . Don't.

ANNE	I can do it.
CHARLOTTE	I don't want you wearing yourself out.
ANNE	What are we supposed to do with all of these?
CHARLOTTE	Read them.
ANNE	We don't have space for all of them.
CHARLOTTE	We can put some in Papa's study. Some in Emily's . . .

Beat.

ANNE	It was kind of your publisher to send these for her.

CHARLOTTE   She didn't have time to read a single one.

*ANNE notices an envelope tucked into one of the crates.
She opens it. Inside is a poster that she unfolds.*

ANNE   *Jane Eyre* . . . As a play? You didn't tell us about this. Why
didn't you go?

CHARLOTTE   It was last month.

ANNE   You could have gone.

CHARLOTTE   No. I couldn't.

CHARLOTTE grabs the poster from out of ANNE's hands.

Papa wants us to go through her room. Decide what
to keep . . . What to give away. We need to change the
sheets . . . Throw out her clothes—

ANNE   Throw them out?

CHARLOTTE   You can keep what you'd like. Anything else we can
give away.

ANNE   What about her bed?

CHARLOTTE   I assumed you would use it.

ANNE   Why?

CHARLOTTE   You'll take her room . . . Won't you?

ANNE   No.

CHARLOTTE	You should. You've been sleeping in Branwell's studio for years now. It's hardly a bedroom.
ANNE	But . . . That room is hers.
CHARLOTTE	And you can have it. She would want you to.
ANNE	I . . . Couldn't.
CHARLOTTE	Well . . . Either way . . . We need to clean it out.
ANNE	Can't we wait? It feels too soon to . . .

Beat.

We waited months before deciding what to do about Bran's—

CHARLOTTE	It will only get harder the longer we . . .

Beat.

I can do it without you . . . If you want. I just thought you would want to be—

ANNE	I do. I do. I just . . .

Beat.

Sometimes I don't know what I'm supposed to do.

Beat.

CHARLOTTE	You stay busy.

CHARLOTTE puts the last pile of books on the shelf.

That's the last of them.

CHARLOTTE takes off her glasses, rubs her eyes.

ANNE   Are you tired?

CHARLOTTE   No. Are you?

ANNE   No.

CHARLOTTE   You should be in bed.

ANNE   I want to be here.

ANNE sits back in the rocking chair.

I've nearly finished the skirt.

CHARLOTTE   You didn't have to do that.

ANNE   I know. Will you read?

CHARLOTTE   I might.

ANNE   Have you written?

CHARLOTTE   No.

ANNE   Will you?

CHARLOTTE   I'm not sure.

CHARLOTTE notices EMILY's writing desk. She goes to the desk and begins to search through it. As she does, she finds something tucked away in the back. She pulls out a few pieces of paper—newspaper clippings.

Did you know she kept these?

ANNE   What?

CHARLOTTE brings the clippings to ANNE.

No. Did you?

CHARLOTTE   No.

ANNE   These are some of the worst ones.

CHARLOTTE grabs the clippings from ANNE, as if to rip them up.

Don't!

CHARLOTTE   I don't want these in the house.

ANNE   They were hers. She cut them herself.

CHARLOTTE   That's not a reason to . . . The way you would get newspapers for her . . . The two of you sitting together . . . Day after day—

ANNE   I wanted her to read the positive reviews when they finally came out.

CHARLOTTE   It didn't matter that they were positive. She kept reading the scathing ones instead. She practically had them memorized.

ANNE	You can't blame us for wanting to know how our work was received. We weren't getting letters and invitations like you were. Other than our reviews, we had no way of knowing what people thought of our novels.
CHARLOTTE	She became obsessed with them. She should have focused on writing . . . On writing another novel. She allowed herself to become completely crippled by—
ANNE	It was hard.
CHARLOTTE	It's been hard for all of us. All of this. It . . .

CHARLOTTE looks at clippings. She thinks about destroying them.

ANNE	Don't.

CHARLOTTE puts them back into EMILY's writing desk. She picks up EMILY's quill.

You should use it.

Beat.

CHARLOTTE	No.

CHARLOTTE puts the quill away.

ANNE	You haven't written in weeks . . .
CHARLOTTE	Anne, I'm fine.
ANNE	She would want you to write. To keep going. To keep going with . . .

CHARLOTTE closes her eyes.

I can help, you know. You can read me your pages. Like we used to. You might feel better. You might feel more at ease if you—

CHARLOTTE   I won't feel . . .

Beat.

It's getting late. It's time for bed.

ANNE   No.

CHARLOTTE   Yes. You need to rest.

ANNE   I want to talk.

CHARLOTTE   There's nothing to discuss.

ANNE   There is.

Beat.

If it had been me . . . If I had been the one who passed—

CHARLOTTE   Oh . . . Anne!

ANNE   Let me finish.

Beat.

If I had been the one who passed . . . And Emily was here . . . Would you speak to her about your work . . . About your—

CHARLOTTE   I don't know.

ANNE   I think you would.

CHARLOTTE   I have no way of knowing what Emily and I would be speaking about.

ANNE   You never talk to me about your work.

CHARLOTTE   I do.

ANNE   When it was the three of us . . . You would always talk to her. It was like it was only the two of you in the room together.

CHARLOTTE   That's not true.

ANNE   It was Emily you wanted to have join you in Brussels. Even though she hated being away from home. She didn't even stay to complete her studies. I would have stayed. I would have graduated.

CHARLOTTE   We only had enough money for two of us to go.

ANNE   You wanted Emily to be part of our collection. You wanted her poems.

CHARLOTTE   I wanted us to publish our work together.

ANNE   You asked me to make all sorts of changes to mine.

CHARLOTTE   We all suggested changes to each other, Anne.

ANNE   And if I hadn't shown you my novel . . . If I hadn't forced you to read *Agnes Grey*?

CHARLOTTE   You didn't force me.

ANNE   Would you have even asked me to publish it?

CHARLOTTE   Yes.

ANNE   But . . . You never . . .

CHARLOTTE   Anne . . . What is it?

              Beat.

ANNE   You've never had anything kind to say about my work . . .
              About my poetry . . . My novels.

CHARLOTTE   It wasn't about being kind. It was about trying to improve
              what we were all—

ANNE   You were always the hardest on me. When we shared our
              work, you would criticize me the most.

CHARLOTTE   I was being constructive.

ANNE   You've never hidden how you feel about my work.

CHARLOTTE   I trusted you could hear my concerns without harbouring
              endless amounts of—

ANNE   You don't like my work. You never have.

CHARLOTTE   Your style is not to my liking. That doesn't mean your work
              isn't . . . You might not like everything that I write either.

ANNE   But I do. I love *Jane Eyre*.

CHARLOTTE	And in time . . . I think you'll find a story that's . . . That's . . .
	Beat.
	You need more time.
ANNE	Time?
CHARLOTTE	Yes. It takes time to—
ANNE	I've had two novels published in the time you've only had one—
CHARLOTTE	Yes. And you never waste an opportunity to remind me of that.
ANNE	*Wildfell Hall* has sold as many copies as when *Jane Eyre* was first—
CHARLOTTE	It hasn't sold as many copies.
ANNE	Nearly. And Helen is a heroine loved just as much as Jane . . . Maybe even more. Reviews praised that book.
CHARLOTTE	And I don't have to agree with every—
ANNE	You couldn't even get your first novel published. No one wanted to publish *The Professor.* They still don't.
CHARLOTTE	It's a difficult novel to sell.
ANNE	Well . . . It's a difficult novel to read too.
CHARLOTTE	Are you finished?

ANNE   You're not better than I am, Charlotte.

CHARLOTTE   I never said I was.

ANNE   You've always acted as if you were.

CHARLOTTE   I'm not going to show you or your work any sort of favou-
                ritism simply because you're my sister.

ANNE   Emily would never treat me the way that you—

CHARLOTTE   Emily and I are not the same.

ANNE   No. You most certainly are not.

CHARLOTTE   Well, maybe you'd be better off if she were here instead
                of me.

                Beat.

ANNE   What?

                Beat.

CHARLOTTE   You were always closer to her. I know that. If you were
                given the choice . . . I know you would choose to have her
                here . . . Instead of me.

ANNE   I could say the same thing about you, couldn't I?

                Beat.

CHARLOTTE   I think it's probably best if we . . .

                Beat.

CHARLOTTE *heads for the door.*

ANNE   I miss her.

                CHARLOTTE stops.

                I miss her so much . . . Sometimes I can't breathe. I find
                myself talking to her . . . I talk to her all the time. As soon
                as I wake up in the morning . . . When I'm lying in bed at
                night . . . When I'm out walking. Any thought that comes
                into my head . . . I want to tell her . . . I want her to know.

                Beat.

                Where do I put it?

CHARLOTTE   What?

ANNE   Her. Where do I put her . . . The feeling of her. I can feel her
                on my skin . . . The smell of her. I hear her voice. I want to
                keep her so close to me. Fit her inside my chest and just . . .

                Beat.

                I don't know what I'm supposed to.

                Beat.

CHARLOTTE   Neither do I.

                Beat.

ANNE   I wasn't ready . . .

CHARLOTTE   Of course not.

ANNE   I know, but . . . And now . . .

              Beat.

              Did we do this to her?

CHARLOTTE   No, Anne. She was sick. Very, very sick.

ANNE   I know. But . . . Did we cause it?

CHARLOTTE   No.

ANNE   Did we make it worse?

CHARLOTTE   How could we possibly have made it—

ANNE   When we went to London . . . She begged us not to go. For
              weeks she begged us not to.

CHARLOTTE   We had to.

ANNE   Did we?

CHARLOTTE   Yes.

ANNE   But if we had just sent a letter explaining instead of going
              in person. Instead of—

CHARLOTTE   It was too important to send a letter.

ANNE   Emily wouldn't even speak to us when we returned. The
              idea of anyone knowing who we are.

CHARLOTTE   Only our publishers know.

ANNE	And Papa.
CHARLOTTE	And Papa. We couldn't keep it from him any longer. But that's all.
ANNE	Still. It was enough to make her sick about it.
CHARLOTTE	She was sick long before we went to London.
ANNE	But when we returned . . . She never recovered. And she hated me.
CHARLOTTE	She didn't hate you.
ANNE	It was never the same between us.
CHARLOTTE	Anne . . .
ANNE	The hardest part is that I had a glorious time on that visit . . . In London. Even now . . . Saying that out loud feels like a complete and utter betrayal.

Beat.

Do you remember the opera?

CHARLOTTE	Yes.
ANNE	I'd never seen so many people in one place. I've thought about that night over and over again. Once . . . I was sitting with her. She was in bed . . . Her breathing was heavy.

She asked me what I was thinking about. And in that moment . . . I was thinking about the costumes . . . The singing. I didn't have the heart to tell her . . . So I said I was thinking about sewing. But I wasn't. I was thinking about that night . . . About the opera.

CHARLOTTE I think about it too.

ANNE Do you?

CHARLOTTE Yes.

ANNE You don't wish that Emily had gone with you on that trip instead of me?

CHARLOTTE No. And Emily couldn't have travelled in her condition. Even if she could . . . Can you imagine her in London?

ANNE She would have been a disaster.

CHARLOTTE She would have panicked the whole trip.

ANNE She wouldn't have left the hotel.

CHARLOTTE She would have been angry with us for going out . . . For being entertained . . . For enjoying ourselves.

ANNE She would have been miserable.

CHARLOTTE The entire trip . . . Yes.

Beat.

ANNE I'd like to go away again.

CHARLOTTE Oh yes?

ANNE Yes.

CHARLOTTE	Where would you like to go?
ANNE	To the seaside. I went for a weekend when I worked for the Inghams. It was beautiful. The sand was so white . . . The sunset was warm . . . The water stretched on for miles and miles.

ANNE closes her eyes.

I want to feel the air in my lungs . . . feel the breeze on my face.

ANNE opens her eyes.

I'm going to go.

CHARLOTTE	We'll see.
ANNE	I don't need your permission.
CHARLOTTE	And I don't need you going there and making yourself . . .

Beat.

We will see if you're well enough to go.

ANNE	Even if I'm not . . . I want to be by the water. Even if it's the last time I . . .

Beat.

Will you come?

CHARLOTTE	Who, me?

ANNE   Yes, you.

CHARLOTTE   You would want me to come?

ANNE   Maybe . . . If you behave.

CHARLOTTE   I always behave.

ANNE   No. Not always.

                They look at each othe and smile.

                Mr. Nicholls was here today. I heard him asking Papa if you
                were home. I think he fancies you.

CHARLOTTE   I'm sure Papa would be thrilled with that.

ANNE   Why wouldn't he be? He seems gentle . . . Kind. He's smart.

CHARLOTTE   He's Papa's curate.

ANNE   So? I've seen you talking with him.

CHARLOTTE   When have you seen that?

ANNE   He's walked you home from church. He always lingers
                around the house to talk to you after he's done with Papa.

CHARLOTTE   He's nice. Friendly.

ANNE   Suppose it doesn't hurt that he's handsome.

CHARLOTTE   He's not that handsome.

ANNE   Oh, yes he is!

They laugh. ANNE *looks at her and smiles.*

CHARLOTTE   What?

Beat.

ANNE   I like the idea of you getting married.

CHARLOTTE   Come now. No one said anything about marriage.

ANNE   I don't want you to be alone.

CHARLOTTE   I'm not alone.

ANNE   I know.

Beat.

I want you to have someone who can take care of you . . .
After I've . . .

Beat.

I don't want you to be here alone.

ANNE *has a tickle in her throat. She tries to clear it.*
CHARLOTTE *looks at her.*

CHARLOTTE   Come . . . I'll make you some warm milk with honey.

ANNE   You haven't made that in ages.

CHARLOTTE   It will be a little treat.

CHARLOTTE *offers* ANNE *her hand.*

ANNE   Will you read to me?

CHARLOTTE   Read?

ANNE   I love hearing you read.

CHARLOTTE   What would you like to hear?

              ANNE stands.

ANNE   Something new. Something of yours.

              They walk toward the door.

CHARLOTTE   Maybe I'll read you something from *Shirley*.

ANNE   *Shirley?*

CHARLOTTE   I think it's the title . . . Of my next novel.

ANNE   Is Shirley the main character?

CHARLOTTE   Yes.

ANNE   What's she like?

CHARLOTTE   Well . . . She's stubborn, difficult, quick—

ANNE   Oh. So . . . Like Emily.

CHARLOTTE   Yes. Like Emily.

              ANNE turns around.

              What?

ANNE looks at the room as if saying goodbye.

Come.

CHARLOTTE kisses ANNE's hand, then leads her out of the room.

POSTLUDE

*CHARLOTTE enters the room. She is dressed in black—
mourning wear.*

*She sits in the rocking chair, feeling the arms of it. She
stands and walks to the window, looks out. She looks
around the room and hears the silence of the house.*

*CHARLOTTE tears up. She weeps. She covers her mouth
so her father doesn't hear.*

*She finally begins to calm herself and wipes her eyes
with her sleeve.*

*She goes to the table and opens her writing desk. She
pulls out paper and sits. She tries to steady her breathing. She stares at a blank page for a moment, then
reaches for a quill. She looks up.*

*EMILY and ANNE are in the room. EMILY looks up at
CHARLOTTE, then ANNE. The three sisters look at each
other. CHARLOTTE is overcome by the memory of them.*

*CHARLOTTE returns to her work. She looks up again
as if to say something, but EMILY and ANNE are gone.*

CHARLOTTE *looks at the paper in front of her. She
breathes heavily.*

Very slowly, she begins to write.

End of play.

A BRONTË CHRONOLOGY

In the play, some historical events have been condensed, combined, and adapted for dramatic purposes.

December 1812
Patrick Brontë, an Irish-born curate working in Yorkshire, marries Maria Branwell.

April 23, 1814
Baptism of their first child, Maria (birthdate unknown).

February 8, 1815
Birth of their second child, Elizabeth.

April 21, 1816
Birth of their third child, Charlotte.

June 26, 1817
Birth of their fourth child, and only son, (Patrick) Branwell.

July 30, 1818
Birth of their fifth child, Emily.

January 17, 1820
Birth of their sixth and last child, Anne.

April 1821
Patrick Brontë becomes perpetual curate of Haworth in West Yorkshire, England. The family moves into the parsonage, which overlooked a church and graveyard.

September 15, 1821
Maria Brontë, Patrick's wife, dies at the age of thirty-eight, probably of uterine cancer.

May 6, 1825
Maria, aged twelve, dies of tuberculosis while away at Roe Head School in Mirfield, twenty miles from Haworth.

June 15, 1825
Elizabeth, aged ten, dies of tuberculosis soon after returning from Roe Head.

July 1835
Charlotte leaves Haworth to become a teacher at her old school, Roe Head. Emily accompanies her as a pupil until she falls ill and returns home. Anne later takes Emily's place.

September 1835
Branwell attends the Royal Academy of Arts in London for a very brief period of time.

May 1838
Branwell goes to Bradford, where he sets up as a portrait painter.

Late September 1838
Emily becomes a teacher at Law Hill School. Anne leaves Roe Head.

December 1838
Charlotte resigns from her teaching job at Roe Head.

March 1839
Emily leaves her teaching job at Law Hill School.

April 1839
Anne is engaged as a governess by the Ingham family of Mirfield.

Mid-May 1839
Branwell gives up his portrait studio and returns to Haworth. Charlotte briefly serves as governess to the Sidgwick family of Stone Gappe.

December 1839
Anne leaves her position with the Inghams.

January 1840
Branwell is engaged as a tutor by the Postlethwaite family of Broughton-in-Furness.

Early May 1840
Anne becomes governess to the Robinson family of Thorpe Green.

June 1840
Branwell is dismissed by the Postlethwaites for drunkenness.

August 1840
Branwell takes a job as assistant clerk at Sowerby Bridge railway station.

March 1841
Charlotte is engaged as a governess by the White family of Rawdon.

February 1842
To improve their foreign language skills in preparation for a plan to open their own school, Charlotte and Emily leave England to study at the Pensionnat Héger in Brussels. Charlotte begins teaching to support herself as a student, and forms an obsessive attachment to Constantin Héger, husband of the school's director.

March 1842
Branwell is dismissed from his job at the railway station.

November 1842
Having learned of the death of their aunt Elizabeth (their mother's sister), Charlotte and Emily leave Brussels for Haworth. Their aunt has left each of the sisters a small inheritance.

January 1843
Branwell joins Anne in the Robinson household, where he has been engaged as a tutor. Charlotte returns to Brussels. Emily does not return to Brussels, deciding to stay in Haworth for good.

January 1844–May 1846
Anne's position as governess to the Robinson family comes to an end. Charlotte leaves Brussels for good. On her return to Haworth, she finds her father's eyesight is failing. Branwell is dismissed in disgrace from his tutoring job at the Robinsons because of an illicit attachment to Mrs. Robinson, which Branwell hoped would lead to marriage after her husband's death. He returns to Haworth. All four siblings are at home with their father.

May 1846
Publication of *Poems* by Currer, Ellis, and Acton Bell—the male pseudonyms adopted by Charlotte (Currer), Emily (Ellis), and Anne (Acton). Only two copies out of a thousand are sold. The book receives three reviews.

August 1846
Charlotte accompanies her father to Manchester to undergo surgery on his eyes.

July 1847
After Mr. Robinson's death, Mrs. Robinson makes it clear to Branwell that she will not marry him. Branwell declines into chronic alcoholism, opiate use, and debt. He sets fire to his bed, causing greater concern for the family.

Winter and Spring 1847
The sisters each finish their first novels: *The Professor* (Charlotte), *Wuthering Heights* (Emily's only novel), and *Agnes Grey* (Anne). The novels are submitted to publishers with the intention that they be published together as one volume.

Summer 1847
The process of publication proceeds for *Wuthering Heights* and *Agnes Grey* only. Charlotte continues to submit *The Professor* but does not secure a publisher. Charlotte receives encouraging response from Smith, Elder & Co., who express an interest in any other work by Currer Bell. Six weeks later, Charlotte completes *Jane Eyre* and the novel is published.

Fall 1847
Jane Eyre becomes a publishing sensation almost immediately, garnering almost universal praise. Critical reception for *Wuthering Heights* is polarized and lukewarm for *Agnes Grey*.

Summer 1848
Speculation is rife about the identities and genders of the mysterious Currer, Ellis, and Acton Bell. To help sell more copies of *Agnes Grey*, Emily and Anne's publisher publicly claims and advertises that it was written by Currer Bell. Charlotte's publisher is furious about the claim.

Fall 1848
Charlotte and Anne visit London to prove to their publishers the existence of separate Bells, revealing for the first time that they are women. Publication of *The Tenant of Wildfell Hall* by Anne, who is still writing as Acton Bell. The book receives more positive reviews than *Agnes Grey*, with specific praise of its protagonist, Helen Graham.

September 24, 1848
Branwell dies of chronic bronchitis (or possibly tuberculosis) at the age of thirty-one.

December 19, 1848
Emily dies of tuberculosis at the age of thirty.

May 28, 1849
Anne and Charlotte take a trip to the seaside at Scarborough, which Anne had visited while working for the Ingham family. While there, Anne dies of tuberculosis at the age of twenty-nine.

October 1849
Publication of *Shirley* by Charlotte, still writing as Currer Bell.

December 1850
A new combined edition of *Wuthering Heights* and *Agnes Grey* contains a "biographical notice" by Charlotte, in which she publicly confirms that the authors were in fact her sisters.

January 1853
Publication (still pseudonymously) of Charlotte's *Villette*.

June 1854
Charlotte marries her father's curate, Arthur Bell Nicholls, who moves into the parsonage to help care for Patrick.

March 31, 1855
At the age of thirty-eight, Charlotte dies of phthisis and possible complications in pregnancy.

June 1857
Posthumous (and still pseudonymous) publication of Charlotte's first—and until now, unpublished—novel, *The Professor*. A preface by her husband is included.

June 7, 1861
Patrick Brontë dies at the age of eighty-four, having outlived his whole family.

ACKNOWLEDGEMENTS

I am deeply indebted to the following people:

To my dramaturg Bob White for shepherding *Brontë: The World Without* from start to finish and for our countless conversations that shaped this script and the world of this play.

To Antoni Cimolino for his belief in me and his encouragement of this project. To Anita Gaffney, David Auster, Jason Miller, David Prosser, Beth Russell, and the team at the Stratford Festival. I am so grateful for all of the work and effort that went into the premiere production.

To the cast and creative team of the premiere production: Beryl Bain, Jessica B. Hill, Andrea Rankin, Narda McCarroll, Kimberly Purtell, Anton de Groot, Kim Lott, and Katherine Dermott. Working with this group of artists was a complete and utter dream.

To Vanessa Porteous for directing the premiere production with such ferocity and for creating a space where we could all strive for the utmost best.

To the artists who lent me their talents during the development of the script: Beryl Bain, Sascha Cole, Jennifer Dzialoszynski, Deborah Hay, Jessica B. Hill, Irene Poole, Andrea Rankin, Laura Schutt, and Julie Tepperman.

To the team at Playwrights Canada Press: Annie Gibson, Blake Sproule, and Jessica Lewis. Thank you for all of the work in bringing this piece to life on the page. To Leah Renihan for her fabulous cover design.

To Sarah Laycock, Amy Rowbottom, and the team at the Brontë Parsonage Museum in Haworth, England. Thank you for spending hours and hours with me as you answered my Brontë questions and gave me a tour of the sisters' home when I visited the museum.

To my agent Ian Arnold for continuing to be my partner in crime.

To the family and friends who gave their love and support along the way: Philip Akin, Lisa Codrington, Sascha Cole, Daryl Fridenberg, Kate Hennig, Jason Mandlowitz, Zachary Mandlowitz, Hannah Moscovitch, and Sabryn Rock.

And to my husband, Marcus Jamin, without whom this play would simply not be possible.

Jordi Mand is a Toronto-based writer for theatre, TV, and film. Her plays include *Between the Sheets, Caught, This Will Be Excellent*, and *Brontë: The World Without*. Her work has been produced nationally and internationally and has been published by Playwrights Canada Press. She is a graduate of the Bell Media Prime TV Program at the Canadian Film Centre and the National Theatre School of Canada. Jordi is a writer on the fourth season of the hit CTV crime drama *Cardinal* and on the upcoming film adaptation of Harriet Alida Lye's thriller *The Honey Farm*.

ition: July 2020

d and bound in Canada by Rapido Books, Montreal

jacket art is a reproduction of Branwell Brontë's untitled portrait of
sisters.
cket design by Leah Renihan
Author photo © David Leyes

PLAYWRIGHTS
CANADA PRESS

202-269 Richmond St. W.
Toronto, ON
M5V 1X1

416.703.0013
info@playwrightscanada.com
www.playwrightscanada.com
@playcanpress